Thinking fast and slow in football

Written by
Kasim farrag

ISBN / 9798227085337

Dedication

To my dear father and dear mother, even if it is a meager attempt to thank them for their continuous sacrifices for me, I do not think that I will find words or actions that match what they have done for me, and therefore this work is the result of your great efforts. I truly thank you.

Also by KASIM FARRAG

Thinking Fast and Slow in Football

Watch for more at https://www.amazon.com/dp/B0DB8HPPJS.

introduction

The study of the human mind has remained, and still is, one of the most difficult studies that scientific research has known throughout the ages. Even though these studies have witnessed great development in recent times in terms of directing the interest of scientific research to how the human mind works and determining its functions, the history of previous studies makes us not We give full confidence to the results of the current studies, and this does not mean that those previous studies failed, but rather it shows us the difficulty of the study and the depth of its details, as the human mind still resembles a large, very dark room. Every study illuminates for us a part that does not represent one of the millions of parts inside that room, even if there are many. Sometimes a strong study is presented on this subject, and it may last for years. Then another study comes along that contradicts and clarifies the errors in that study and builds a new study. Thus, the study of the human mind represents the most difficult studies known to scientific research throughout its great and enormous history with regard to this subject, as it was presented to us. Previous studies are a good legacy that we can navigate through with great care. Studies of the human mind have contributed to tremendous development in various fields of life such as economics, sociology, psychology, natural sciences, and sports sciences. However, sports sciences, especially football training, have noticeably lacked recently in the efforts of studies. Research that can provide explanations and results becomes scientific theories through which we can develop players' mental abilities and thus develop basic and individual skills and tactical performance, as most athletes in the field of football training are interested in developing physical aspects, the results of which have appeared clearly in recent years and which can be observed by the viewer who follows football matches. From the period of the nineties until now, this viewer can also notice the skill sterility, whether at the level of basic skills or individual skills, which has occurred recently as a result of neglecting the development of the skill

and tactical aspects. **However, in this book the matter will be somewhat different from what is usual in books. Sports training, where attention is focused on how to develop the mind of players in proportion to skill, tactical, and physical performance as well. In this book, we will learn about the functions of the human mind, the characteristics of each function and its capabilities, how to develop them through football training, and how to develop training programs to develop them through which one can Football players develop their basic and individual skills, and through it coaches can also build training plans that enhance the players' mental, skill, tactical and physical abilities in an effective and powerful way .**

Keys to drawing exercises

Pass the ball yellow arrow

Player running without ball Black Arrow

Player running with the ball white arrow

Player's position without the ball

The player's focus on the ball

Players' shirt numbers and balls

Cones

Chapter I
Fast thinking

Introduction

Before starting to talk about quick thinking, we must define the human mind so that we can understand its functions well.

Here we present a group of concepts that scientists have studied and analyzed. Psychologists define the mind as: - the total sum of conscious and unconscious mental processes. The human mind is the symbol of human thinking and the mechanism by which mental processes are attributed It is clear from the previous definitions that a person has only one mind, except that this mind has two functions that are different from each other, as each of them has different functions and characteristics from the other. Over the course of previous studies that focused on studying the human mind, scientists did not differ much in the essence of the two functions that the mind was assigned to, as studies They are very similar in what they discussed regarding the characteristics and functions of each, and the difference arises in the names of each without affecting the essence of the study, as those names were used to differentiate between the two functions, and among those names are the conscious mind and the subconscious mind, the awake mind and the sleeping mind, the voluntary mind and the voluntary mind. Involuntary thinking, fast thinking and slow thinking, and since the purpose of this book is to describe and develop the two functions of the mind in the field of football, which is one of the most important popular sports in the majority of countries in the world, and has even

become part of the economy of some countries, especially Brazil and Argentina, and the great financial returns that return to those countries. In parallel with the professionalism of its children in the majority of international leagues, I therefore prefer the term "fast thinking" and "slow thinking" to describe the mental functions of athletes in football, as these terms are the best due to their closeness and description of what happens in football in terms of fast and slow decisions, movements and running on the field during training and local and international competitions. I do not hide news from you, dear reader.

When I turned my attention to studying this topic and began researching and reviewing many different studies, I did not find an introduction that explained and described the importance of studying the functions of the mind better than the one presented by Dr. (Joseph Murphy)

He likened the human mind to a garden, and through-out the day you sow seeds (ideas) in rapid thinking, and most of the time this is without your awareness, because these seeds are based on your habitual thinking, and through it, the harvest of those seeds (ideas) will

be in your entire mental, psychological, social, and health life... etc Therefore, quick thinking is fertile soil in which all seeds grow, no matter how

good or bad they are. He is not aware of what you give him, but he retains and strengthens what you give him. Therefore, if you sow thorns, you will not reap roses or fruits, since if you plant positive and correct thoughts and strengthen them in a way that suits the capabilities of quick thinking, and the training is done. It is done well in proportion to the capabilities of that fast think-ing. The result will be good in any case and under any circumstances of training and competition. The end of the plot is that the relationship between fast and slow thinking is a direct relationship, as the better your con-scious abilities (slow thinking) are in choosing what is appropriate. One of the thoughts that comes to him during training and competition

The outcome of quick thinking will be more efficient and positive in issuing appropriate responses to each of the different playing situations....

The concept of quick thinking

The concept of quick thinking : - It is a storage room for everything that passes through the mind that no longer exists in the mind Conscious thinking (slow thinking), which includes all decisions related to the individual's previous

experiences, beliefs, memories, and all the situations he experiences and the images he sees in his life.

Another concept of fast thinking

It is a thinking process in which the mind uses multiple techniques to make decisions and solve Problem solving quickly. It depends on previous experience, sense of self, and thinking through imagination and creativity. Rapid thinking refers to the mental process that takes place quickly and without mental effort or with low effort.

Another concept of quick thinking

It is the ability to think and make decisions quickly, including assessing the situation and reaching conclusions To resolve quickly and is often associated with emergency situations where the individual needs to respond quickly to prevent harm as well as working during normal situations in daily life.

Through these concepts, it becomes clear to us that this thinking is automatic, meaning that it works without our control, and that it is also characterized by speed in making decisions in the various situations to which it is exposed, and that it does not depend on exerting great mental effort, as it works with low effort and

in an automatic manner, and that it bases many of its decisions based on impressions. emotions and feelings,

For example, when you see a person whose features appear angry, as in the picture, you are without the need for deep thinking or mental effort, and as a result of prior experiences stored in memory and impressions of such a situation, you can

know that it is a picture of an angry person.

This shows that this thinking has a set of characteristics that distinguish the type of work it does and how it does it. In order to understand a broader and more comprehensive understanding of the concept of quick thinking, we must quickly set out to learn about its characteristics, which explain to us a lot of information about this type of thinking.

Characteristics of quick thinking

Through the previous concepts of rapid thinking, the picture has become clear to us that this type of thinking has a set of features that explain how it works, its

controls, and the functions that it performs, which prompted us to learn about it and study it so that we can be aware of and have a deeper understanding of rapid thinking that helps us become familiar with its capabilities and properties that will and will During her studies that

We know how our mind works while performing in football, which allows us to develop our scientific abilities in a practical scientific way, away from the theoretical aspects that we cannot benefit from in the way required to develop our mental abilities. Therefore, let us quickly discuss the characteristics, capabilities and functions of quick thinking through study and analysis.

Fast thinking is automatic and intuitive

As we explained in the previous concept, quick thinking represents the random memory of the human mind, as it includes everything that the individual has gone through in terms of experiences, experiences, different situations, and images. As long as these things are present within that memory, it is not difficult for fast thinking to retrieve those situations, experiences, and images quickly

and easily. Fast thinking depends on simple mental rules that do not engage in deep thinking and tends to intuition, as things appear to us to be correct when theyfit the basic mental rule. Therefore, decisions are fast and intuitive for us, and fast thinking depends on linking old ideas stored in random memory. And the new ideas that we are exposed to, and therefore he makes the suggestions that we make, no matter how much they seem correct to us according to our experiences and feelings, but we must also take into account that slow thinking is monitoring those suggestions, and while if they are out of the ordinary for him, he rejects them and adopts managing the situation and providing... appropriate solutions,

for example

You can automatically and quickly recognize the picture of one of the people who studied with you at the university level, several years after graduation, even if it was among a group of people in a public place. In such a situation, quick thinking

depends on recalling old pictures and situations that used to bring you together.

You can also solve the mathematical problem $3 + 3 = 6$ without having to exert any mental effort or taking a long time. Considering that you have gone through all stages of education, starting from basic education until the end of university education, it is necessary that you have

studied the basic operations in mathematics such as addition, subtraction, and division, and for this reason Simple problems like this one

will not require mental effort from you, and your answers will be very fast.

Another example

You can also distinguish the sounds that you are accustomed to hearing, even if you are in the middle of a large party, such as the voice of one of your relatives or the voice of a singer whose songs you are accustomed to hearing. Likewise, even if you are deep in sleep, you can identify the type of sound.

Notice the sound that bothered you when it is a familiar sound from the environment in which you live, such as the sound of the television, the sound of an alarm clock, or the sound of a car outside.

Also, you can easily distinguish the feelings of anger, joy, and fear in others from the first glance at them.

Important note

(During the narration throughout the book, you will find many illustrative examples of each element. We first mention illustrative examples from outside football, as they relate to life in general, and then they are followed by illustrative examples from within football, and this is not

Not only to simplify the information, but in order to emphasize that football is based on distortion and professionalism, where no one can see... Development Through the field only, but it is necessary to extend it It goes beyond this field to include all parts of the player's life Yt He can reach meto the desired performance).

(Illustrative examples through football) First example

During one of the matches, one of the players of the opposing team obstructed your teammate within the boundaries of the opposing team's penalty area, and when you noticed it, the referee blew his whistle and pointed with his hand as in the picture. You very automatically and without the need to exert mental effort, you can realize that the referee has awarded a penalty kick in favor of your team as a result of the obstruction. One of the players to your colleague within

the boundaries of the opposing team's penalty area, as such a situation exists in

several forms within the random memory of the mind, which is one of the elements of forming quick thinking, as it is possible that it was recorded on the basis of your study of football law or through experiences and practice of the game and etc. The important thing in the end is that quick thinking was able

to respond to the situation without the need for a long time or any significant mental effort.

Second example

If you were playing in the defense position and during the match, one of the opposing team's attackers, while you were chasing him when he was alone with your team's goalkeeper, eluded the goalkeeper, but for some reason, such as losing his balance, he shot the ball weakly

towards the goal. You can catch the ball if you increase your speed and then slide to distract the ball. Ball: I do not think that your

assessment of the situation at this moment, which will not take a fraction of a second, will make you neglect to catch up

With the ball, you will rush with all speed to try to prevent the ball from entering the goal, as your experiences, information stored in your random memory,

And your feeling say that you have the ability to do this, or even trying is sufficient, which has a probability equal to or exceeding 50%.

Third example

When you perform a direct shot at the opposing team's goal, notice that you pay attention to the exaggerated exit of the opposing team's goalkeeper. This will also be automatic, as your attention to the goalkeeper's incorrect exit and the distance he left behind him, as well as your sense of your position on the field and your appreciation of your ability to perform the shot well will not allow you to think about it too much.

Rather, automatically and with great speed, you will quickly shoot directly at the goal to score a goal. Many situations are similar to

that situation in football, where the reaction is automatic and fast, and does not require mental **eff**ort or low effort.

Fourth example

During one of the matches that you play with your team, if one of your teammates performs a long pass such that you will not be able to reach it, even if you run at your maximum speed, as shown in the picture, then it is obvious and automatically that you will stop catching the ball because you were able to easily estimate the distance between you. And between the ball and that this thing you did was not in vain, but rather the result of your understanding of the properties of the ball and your speed in advance through practice. Previously, this often happens in reverse during the budding stage and the first years of the youth stage, where the lack of experience increases the number of errors related to estimating distances as a result of a lack of good understanding of the properties of the ball, as well as their abilities in terms of speed, strength and endurance, where you find the youth running after a ball that is difficult to catch once. Or he jumped to the top to try to hit the ball with his head, even though the ball is high in the air, where it is difficult to reach it. As we are approaching this point, I would like to point out to you one of the important points.Often in every team we find a player who is distinguished by his ability to perform long passes very well compared to his teammates. In every team he is called the passer.Here is the first question: Is this performance innate or largely acquired, allowing us to develop and train all team members? If it is acquired, then why are current training methods unable to address this problem,

which has become a major dilemma for many players and which has greatly affected

performance in football??? Leave this question now, as you will find the answer in the next pages of the book. I will remind you of it, and let us complete the characteristics of quick thinking now.

Rapid thinking is involuntary

One of the characteristics of rapid thinking is that it is involuntary, meaning that you cannot stop it. It works all the time and always issues responses to everything that occurs to it. Science estimates that 59% of our brain activity is unconscious. This means that the majority of the decisions and behaviors that we take and the actions that we take. Our emotions also depend on quick thinking, not slow thinking, which depends on exerting mental effort by engaging in thinking processes that require reasoning, logic, and scientific arguments. Fast thinking works through information, knowledge, experiences, attitudes, thoughts, and feelings that are stored in random memory and can be accessed. Involuntarily or without making any mental effort, when the name of an international club is mentioned, let it be Real Madrid, you cannot stop your quick thinking about the heroics and legends of Real Madrid, especially the star Cristiano Ronaldo. Also, for example, when you hear the sound of a train or a car, you cannot stop your quick thinking. By determining the direction and type

of sound that occurred in the place you are in, this means that the first attention that occurs as a result of any stimulus that occurs to you is involuntary, meaning that you are unable to control the response that occurs. However, after that, you can ignore the source of the sound or continue following it after the first response. Controlling this is considered one of the characteristics of slow thinking, and therefore one of the components of the relationship between fast and slow thinking is controlling attention and controlling it.

Another example: You cannot stop your quick thinking from recognizing the color of a house you just saw while walking on a city street. Therefore, many companies use advertisements on electronic billboards in the streets, as advertising designers know the extent to which this affects people through their lack of control over their quick thinking. Therefore, if the advertisement is somewhat distinctive, it will be stored in their random memory, thus increasing the possibility of purchasing the product promoted through advertisements on electronic boards.

Another example: While you are driving a car on a road, when you encounter a car advancing towards you at a high speed and suddenly, you, without voluntarily or thinking about it and without taking notice, try to avoid that car in order to avoid any collision

with it, especially since your quick thinking possesses prior information and knowledge. About the consequences of a two-car accident, so he carries out

his mission without having to return to slow thinking and analyzing the situation or

entering into logical thinking calculations and the time it takes, as the situation does not require any delay, otherwise the result will not be positive,

especially since such a situation has been analyzed in advance. Before slow thinking and it was stored in random memory in fast thinking, such situations, which do not need the advantage of time and are characterized by direct danger that may expose the

hypothesis to danger, must be dealt with through quick thinking.

(Illustrative examples through football) First example

If you play as a defender and you, along with your teammates, prepare the attack from the back line through short passes, then when you face high pressure and are surrounded by the opposing team's attackers and you do not find a place to pass to one of your teammates, then you unwittingly either scatter the ball or return it to the goalkeeper. Your team, in order to avoid mistakes. Such a situation occurs involuntarily as a result of a sense of danger, the possibility of losing the ball, which may get you into a problem that may cost your team a goal

Second example

Good awareness of information and knowledge in advance and storing it in random memory also often causes involuntary rapid thinking among players.

For example, when one of the opposing team's attackers passes or shoots the ball so that it is as high as below your chest, you are trying to prevent the ball, but you are also involuntarily trying to avoid the ball colliding with your arm, especially if the ball is within the boundaries of the penalty area.

Third example

If you are playing in the striker position and you are dribbling the defender and you notice that the goalkeeper's movements are incorrect, as he is focusing on the foot closest to you, then, without voluntarily, as a result of your knowledge of the laws of sports mechanics, you will perform a direct shot towards the angle of the foot that is not centered on the goalkeeper.

This demonstrates that the information and theoretical knowledge that the player receives affects On voluntary and involuntary some performances in football (A picture shows the attacker taking advantage of the goal-keeper's incorrect movements and his

focus, which made the attacker not think about the matter, but rather, unwittingly, he shot directly at the goal)

Fast thinking is characterized by the ability to perform more than one task at a time

One of the characteristics of quick thinking is its ability to perform more than one task at a time, but on the condition that these tasks are not complex, as they do not require great mental effort, and that these tasks are characterized by simplicity and clarity. It is also necessary that

These tasks passed over slow thinking and became understandable and clear to fast thinking, as they were stored in the random memory that represents fast thinking, which includes experiences, situations, images, feelings, and everything that a person has experienced or even has anything to do with what is present within that memory, where he can think quickly with this. How to deal with more than one stimulus at a time. This is in contrast to slow thinking, which cannot consciously focus on two things at the same time, as the brain gives nervous attention to one thing. This is due to slow thinking requiring great mental effort to deal with the situations to which we are exposed. Which imposes on us the inability to pay attention and focus on more than one stimulus at a time. As for rapid thinking, as we mentioned, it deals with situations that do not require mental effort or require a small effort that does not

affect our ability to pay attention and focus on more than one stimulus at a time. At one time, as it does not deal with situations that are stressful to think about or require intense concentration that makes us lose sight of what is clear and obvious.

for example

You can watch TV while talking to your friend who is sitting next to you without there being any trouble while doing so, as the situation does not require a great deal of mental effort. Another example is that you can drive a car and talk on the phone at the same time when the road is not crowded and quiet in such a matter. You Do not make a lot of mental effort, as driving a car has become simple over time, so it will not require a lot of mental effort.

(Illustrative examples in football) First example

When you receive the ball without any real pressure from the players of the opposing team (negative pressure), you can run with the ball, monitor the movements of teammates and direct them, as well as monitor the movements of the players of the opposing team by doing continuous visual scanning while you are in possession of the ball. Quite the opposite, the majority of players

cannot do a visual scanning. Continuously monitoring the movements of colleagues and competitors and running with the ball correctly with a clear goal when under strong pressure from the players of the opposing team. The idea here lies in the difficulty of the tasks and not in their multiplicity, as the more the tasks are not difficult or complex, you can do it easily and conveniently, but when the matter is More difficult and more complex tasks, this requires greater mental effort, and this is not a characteristic of quick thinking

Second example

Very often, fatal mistakes occur by defenders by not controlling the offside line while defending against a competitor's attack.

This often happens due to the inability of quick thinking of one of the defenders to deal with more than one task at one time as a result

of the inefficiency of quick thinking to deal with it. With more than one difficult task at a time, which is sometimes interpreted as a lack of experience in the player, and this interpretation is wrong. Rather, we can say that the way in which the player was trained was wrong, as quick thinking cannot give the correct effort except by providing him with the correct information and knowledge, as we mentioned previously. If you sow thorns, you will not reap roses. This is why it is necessary to train players' quick thinking to deal with

more than one difficult task at a time, so that during matches the players will be proficient in dealing with more than one

difficult playing situation at the same time.

Rapid thinking is characterized by its tendency toward impressions and feelings

Impressions and feelings are considered one of the pillars upon which rapid thinking is formed and created. Many of the involuntary responses and decisions adopted by rapid thinking are under the influence of impressions and feelings.

Here we must explain the concept of impression well so that we can understand what quick thinking offers in this case

The concept of impression: - (Duha Abdel Khaleq) says that an impression is an idea, opinion, or feeling formed about a thing, a person, or a group, and it is most likely that it was built on foundations that lack evidence and documentation and that it occurred over a period of not a short period and without thinking.

Through this definition, it becomes clear to us that impression contains irrational or emotional decisions and responses that were formed in a circumstantial situation and unconsciously.

Therefore, many of his estimates may be wrong in some different situations, as his decisions are often not according to clear standards or are devoid of impressions and feelings. Therefore, we may find that many of the players' decisions in football during competitions tend to have some of their decisions influenced by some of the impressions they have, which often arise as a result of situations. A past that the player was exposed to left certain impressions on him, or the player was influenced by the media and social media in terms of a particular player, club, audience, or administration, and that naturally leaves him with some impressions and feelings about that, or the players were influenced by the way the coach explained to them about some technical points regarding the player or team.

A certain effect, which leaves a clear impact on the players' decisions during future competitions, or this impression may form within a single team, where one of them may have been affected.

Players from the reactions of a teammate or many mistakes, whether defensive or offensive, repeated over a long period, which leaves a negative impact on a teammate later.

This also shows us that not every impression is wrong, but we also cannot manage our decisions, whether in life in general or within. The field during matches through the impression that may be right or wrong in many cases. This is for

example and not limited to, as there are many situations on the basis of which we form a certain impression as a result of the impact of those situations on ourselves, so let us give some examples outside the sports environment first, then Then we list some situations within

the sports community that show us how our quick thinking is affected by the impression that is produced with the passage of different experiences and situations during our lives outside and inside the sports community.

First example

When you decide to take a trip to a specific city by car to carry out an errand or to enjoy spending your free time, and while you are talking to your friend, he tells you to pay attention while driving the car because the road you will take is naturally dangerous, this makes you have a bad impression of that road, which makes you be very careful while driving the car to the point. It may make you slow down the speed at which you normally drive the car to avoid making mistakes while driving, and this shows the extent of the impact of impressions on your decisions while driving during yourtrip.

Second example

During our childhood, we all read or heard the famous story that told us about the young man who was swimming in the sea towards the shore, then he started screaming and waving his hand to pretend that he was drowning, which made his friends rush to try to save him, and when they reached him, he started laughing and saying that he was joking with them, and he repeated that several times, but the shock was What happened at the end of the story is that this young man was actually drowning, and when he shouted and waved his hand for his friends to save him, none of them paid attention to him, and as a result he died. In fact, the friends did not fail in trying to save him, but his constant joking in this situation left the impression that he was joking a lot and that he He did not drown, which caused a disaster in the end, and this, if this indicates anything, indicates the seriousness of the impressions that tend towards emotion and feeling that form towards different situations.

(Illustrative examples through football) First example

For example, before the end of the season in the league championship, when you face one of the teams that has been able to prove throughout the tournament since the beginning of the season that it is good at pressing the opponent from the front line in a strong way,

and all the teams, fans, and media professionals are talking about that. Naturally, that will raise the impression on you and your colleagues. Which may negatively affect your ability to build the game from the back line. Although you may have found this to be effective in previous matches, the impression you have of this team may cause problems in the passing and movements you make, and this often happens even with big teams. Which pays close attention to the psychological aspects (you can see this through all the matches that Manchester City, led by Pep Guardiola, plays with the big teams, where you find many mistakes during preparation by the teams that face it as a result of the

high pressure that the team puts on sometimes and as a result of the impression that overwhelms the competitors at other times.

In many cases, the opposing team has the ability to build a good attack from the back line, but the influence of the prevailing impression of the Manchester City team, led by the magician Guardiola, is stronger and causes many problems in the process of passing, movement, and tactical performance.

Second example

The impression may also affect the quick-thinking decisions of players within one team. For example, your constant impression, which is created through many situations, towards one of your fellow attackers is that he is not good at dealing with situations in which there are one-on-one situations when facing the goalkeepers of competing teams, where he often fails.

In scoring goals (he is not good in situations alone with the goalkeeper and scoring goals), when you are put to the test of either passing to him or to another striker colleague, without

needing except the trouble of slow thinking, you will pass to the other teammate. This is not only the case, but the matter may develop to

the point that you are in Some of the playing situations in which your pass may be unique to the goalkeeper of the opposing team, except that you may prefer to shoot or dribble the defender and then shoot.

Likewise, the impression of the goalkeeper on the team that one of his fellow defenders is proficient in the skill of passing the ball from the back line to the midfield and leading the attack with excellent effectiveness. This impression affects the goalkeeper's quick-thinking decisions of the necessity of passing to that defender every time the playing situations allow for this, and the bad thing about it is that this He may waste good opportunities for a long pass or even to one of his fellow defenders on the team, or this may be affected by the goalkeeper not appreciating the different playing situations that defender is in every time the ball is passed to him, which may cause him to fall under strong pressure that causes him to lose the ball, resulting in He poses a threat to the team's goal

Third example

If the team you are in will play a match outside the country with one of the teams in the Champions League, and a certain period before the match, the refereeing team that will lead the management of the match has been determined. It is known and common about the first referee that he often deals with colored cards (yellow and red) in many cases.

Playing situations where he does not miss a game, small or

large, unless he uses administrative penalties. Naturally, this will affect your interventions in every game situation for fear of counting any cards against you, whether they are yellow or red.

The same example as before, but the matter is different this time as it concerns the second referee (the flag referee), as he is known to be not good at controlling the offside line. This matter will naturally make you question most of his decisions related to controlling the offside line.

Fourth example

Your prior impression during the league championship matches of the team you are facing in the match that it is not good at dealing with high balls, whether cross or longitudinal, will affect the quick-thinking decisions of the team's wingers and attacking midfielders, which will make them increase their length and cross high balls in order to exploit that smallness in the goalkeeper. The goalkeeper and the defenders, and this is a very good thing, but it may have a negative impact in that if some balls were used, for example, in ground passes, whether longitudinal or transverse, direct shooting, or dribbling, and then shooting, the scoring chances would become higher and stronger, and this shows the extent of the impact of the impression on decisions. Our quick thinking, whether positive or negative, makes us not trust many quick-thinking

decisions that are affected by impressions that may be right or wrong. This is why it is necessary for coaches to take into account how to influence players' impressions in a positive way through good guidance of the way players think about life in general and in life. The field, whether in training or competition in particular, and this will be discussed in detail by talking about how to develop quick thinking among players

Fast thinking is characterized by the fact that it does not stop and works all the time

Our rapid thinking does not rest or take a rest, as modern science shows us that we hear and process everything, even during sleep, and this is what shows us that our rapid thinking works all the time, just as we during the time when we areWhen we are awake, we find that quick thinking processes and presents suggestions and decisions for most of the situations and events that we experience during the day. When we wake up, we can easily determine what to eat for breakfast without the need to exert more mental effort, as each of us has specific and specific types of foods according to his desire. He has a healthy culture and is accustomed to eating it and diversifying it throughout the days, as well as going to work and dealing with colleagues, and even the nature of the work. With the passage of time and the accumulation of experiences, there is no need for great mental effort, as quick thinking during our day takes over, and even situations that exceed his ability, he presents to them. Quick Suggestions

Here, quick thinking intervenes and either approves them or takes over. Likewise, in football during matches, quick thinking does not stop making suggestions and making most decisions during various playing situations that do not require great mental effort or require intense concentration.

(Some illustrative examples through football)

First example

During the match, your quick thinking does not stop working, as there are more responses and suggestions during different playing situations.

When you take possession of the ball, you find your mind preoccupied with more than one suggestion, whether long passing, short passing, or running with the ball. You find quick thinking working all the time in this way, and this is even when The playing situations are more difficult, as he does not leave the matter to the slow thinking directly. He tries to provide solutions for that situation, and the slow thinking either approves of them or rejects them.

Second example

When preparing for an upcoming match, quick thinking responds to this, as it begins to provide responses and suggestions, whether during training or at home. Likewise, during the match, it will respond to every game situation, and after the match as

well, whether the result is victory or defeat, as it does not stop working, even during sleep, as some indicate. Studies have shown that listening to affirmations during sleep affects you in a different way compared to listening to them while awake, as the moment a person sleeps, many biological processes occur in the brain, where new memories are stored while unnecessary information is removed. Therefore, affirmations during sleep help quick thinking. Reprogramming better, and what helps in this is that during sleep we are out of consciousness, which makes every word received by rapid thinking certain.

Rapid, illogical thinking is characterized by

Fast thinking has a set of rules, priorities, coping mechanisms, and emotional reactions that are the result of the situations and experiences that we go through during our lives. Fast thinking depends on repetition, affirmation, feeling, and beliefs.

It does not depend on logic in thinking, unlike slow thinking, and for this reason it derives responses and suggestions from feeling and previous experiences.

And beliefs, which may make or break an opinion. For example, if you know that the person you are talking to is a liar through the previous situations in which you talked to him, then when he comes to talk to you about something, you will not believe what he says, even if he is telling the truth, and you will tend to feel that he is lying. This shows that Rapid thinking depends on feeling, emotion, beliefs, and previous experiences stored in random memory, not thinking logically about the situations and events to which it is exposed.

Example for clarification

We often see in the media and social media many situations in which people justify their political positions or even their affiliation to a football team in illogical ways. This matter is often due to the feeling or belief that the individual believes in, whether on the level of politics, football, or different life situations in general. This is due to either the implicit bias that may arise in us as a result of previous experiences and situations, or through emotional influences, which are deeply intertwined with the decision-making process, as they may overwhelm our rational decisions that are derived from deep thinking. This shows us that the way we program and train quick thinking is... Where practices and controlling emotions dominate our way of life.

(Illustrative examples through football) First example

When you have the ball in the middle of the field and you have the option of passing either to the right wing or... The left wing and we were very similar in positioning, but you feel that the left wing will not dribble and shoot well, so you pass to the right wing. We are often exposed to such a situation on the field, where we have the task of choosing between two or three things, and here in many cases the ruling stems from feeling and belief. And the experiences are not logical, as when you review the video of the match, you can see

that some of the passes you make are illogical, and we say that when you do that and you see through the video that the number of decisions you make are illogical, then it is necessary to review your quick thinking programming, and this is what we will discuss below. he is coming.

Rapid thinking is characterized by dealing with situations and events literally

Fast thinking does not have the ability to scrutinize and reflect on the information it receives. Therefore, it receives information from slow thinking. It accepts it as it is, whether it is true or false, and translates it into experiences and events.

Continuous thinking by slow thinking of some wrong ideas results in wrong translation and suggestions from Before fast thinking and vice versa, where fast thinking takes things as they are, that is, as slow thinking approves of them and adopts them. Therefore, it cannot differentiate between good and evil or between good and bad thoughts. Rather, it believes and responds to what slow thinking believes, and this matter, if you do not know it, is in It is extremely dangerous, because we often think about some situations in ways that are not correct or we misestimate them. In these situations, quick thinking adopts our ideas, believes in them, and responds according to them. This is a cause for concern because of the responses and suggestions it provides later that may make us commit mistakes that cost us a lot in our lives. On the other hand, which is the positive side at this point, because of the belief of fast thinking in the ideas that slow thinking presents to it, it produces for us a stream of responses, suggestions, and reactions that would change our lives for the better. For example, but not limited to, when you think

positively about the fact that you can work from... In order to get more money in

order to buy a new car, you need it. In this case, quick

thinking adopts the idea, believes in it, and begins issuing and presenting creative suggestions in order for you to reach high levels in your work in order to obtain the appropriate money in order to buy the car, and the more The more positive your thinking is, the more creative the ideas are.

This is why we repeat the saying : If you plant roses, you will reap roses, and if you plant thorns, you will not reap grapes. This

is to resemble something that is closer to how quick thinking works.

Another example to clarify

During the study period, the more positive your thoughts are, and you see yourself as a diligent student who can obtain final grades in all academic subjects in order to achieve your dream and reach the university level that you desire. Repeating such positive thoughts makes quick thinking provide you with many suggestions that It helps you organize your time and utilize everything to achieve that goal.

It is the same thing when you think that the mathematics subject that all students complain about is difficult, but for you it is an easy and enjoyable subject and that it helps you develop your mental abilities. That impression, which is led by your slow thinking through its ability to understand mathematics, leads your quick thinking abilities to provide suggestions and solutions. When you study, even if something is

difficult for you while you are studying,

it makes your mood more lively and positive and keeps away negative thoughts that will not be in your dictionary as

long as your slow thinking presents the good and positive belief, so your fast thinking

The one who accepts ideas as they are without thinking about them, whether they are positive or negative. This matter, if you can understand it, may help you change your life for the better always.

(Illustrative examples through football) First example

If, for example, you play in the center-back position, and a week before a match, the team's technical director asks you to review some videos of the striker whom you will be monitoring during the match, and while watching those videos with the coach, you saw through the coach's analysis and your point of view that this striker possesses unique capabilities. In terms of movements, positions, interventions,

head strikes, and special skills, of course, the understanding and interpretation adopted by your slow thinking is reflected in the performance of your quick thinking through the automatic reactions and suggestions it provides.

If the explanations of slow thinking are positive in terms of your ability to control the danger of the attacker, then most of the suggestions The reactions will be balanced and more accurate. However, if the interpretations of slow thinking indicate that this attacker is difficult to stop and that you believe that he will cause you great inconvenience during the match, then fast thinking will also present unbalanced and confused reactions and more mistakes and tension.

Therefore, it is It is necessary to work on the positive points during training and theoretical lectures that depend on performance analyzes of competitors, meaning if the performance analysis shows, for example, that the striker is good at dribbling, it is better to say that it is necessary that I do not leave him the opportunity and space to receive the ball. This is in contrast to saying that it is If he is good at evasion, he will cause me great inconvenience, and this shows that the method you use to think based on it builds results, whether positive or negative. Therefore, the way of thinking either leads us to think quickly to creativity and excellence, or it causes more pain.

Chapter II
Slow thinking

The concept of slow thinking

It is the side that controls perception, analysis, logical and mathematical thinking, and decision-making

Rational decisions consist of two parts: induction and deduction, and inductive thinking is linked to analytical processes

Judgment, choice, and the thinking process express the conscious mind, which here represents slow thinking. It also uses deductive functions that distance itself from thinking.

Therefore, slow thinking is your objective mind and has no memory and can only retain one thought at a time

Slow thinking is also known as

It is a mental process that takes place slowly and requires great effort and high concentration Which a person does when he needs to solve a complex problem or wants to make an important decision.

It is clear from the previous concepts of slow thinking that it depends on mental activities that require mental effort in dealing with various situations that require it, as needed.

It also requires preparation and attention so that it can deal well with situations and activities that require it,

as it is clear from the previous concepts that His work is not easy, as he always performs several activities in order to complete his work in the required manner according to the activities and situations that he deals with. Among the mental activities that he performs to accomplish the tasks are attention, concentration, analysis, conclusion, selection, and making decisions with strength and care that suit each situation in a logical manner.

Example for clarification

For example, if someone asks you to solve a mathematical problem 9+1 = ...

Naturally, it did not take you more than a second or fractions of a second to know that it was an addition problem and that the result is (6), and it did not require you to exert any mental effort to some extent.

But what if the same person asked you to solve the following problem 941 x 323 = ...

Of course, if you do not encounter this problem with the same numbers and you know the result in advance,

the matter will be different from the previous problem, as it will take longer and make a lot of mental effort compared to the previous problem to reach

the correct result, as you will review the mathematical operations that are used to solve such a problem.

The second problem represents slow thinking in that at first you realized that it was a mathematical problem, then your memory began to decline, and when you did not find the solution present in your random memory, you began to focus and began to review the mathematical operations that are used to solve the problem, which forced you to make a mental effort and made you feel that you are making a great effort. compared to the issue

The first until I was able in the end, through review and analysis, I was able to reach the result, which often took longer than the result I reached when solving the first problem. Therefore, it is called slow thinking.

Another example to clarify

Although you may be good at driving cars and it has become easy for you, when a situation on one of the roads requires you to park your car in a narrow area of

13 x 24 = ...

In this situation, you are required to pay attention, focus, and make a mental effort in order to appreciate the space well

Another example to clarify

When you focus on a specific person in the middle of a crowd of people at the train station, this requires you to exert greater mental effort through the attention and focus that you exert.

Illustrative examples through football First example

The attacking players perform a series of short passes in succession in narrow spaces to reach the opposing team's goal, amidst solid and conscious defensive blocks by the defenders, who carry out this defensive work with attention and high concentration. I do not think that the matter will be easy, but rather it requires that work in order to reach the team's goal. The opponent of each of the attackers must pay attention and focus, and make a continuous visual scan with every move he makes, whether before or after receiving, to determine the movements of teammates and defenders, the speed and accuracy of the ball, analyze the playing situation in terms of space and positions, and make the appropriate decision that he implements with every pass he performs from the total number of passes that he performs. It is carried out during the attack, and this work, which imposes on every attacker the use of attention, concentration, analysis, conclusion, choice, and making various decisions during the attack, and the exhaustion of great mental effort by each attacker, represents slow thinking.

Second example

When you execute a direct free kick from an appropriate distance on the edge of the penalty area, you use slow thinking in that you use directed attention to identify the gap in the position of the human wall consisting of the opposing team's defenders and the goalkeeper's position. Then you analyze each and estimate the distance and what is the appropriate speed and height for the ball. It is appropriate whether the ball will be above the wall or on its high sides, as well as the force of kicking the ball. Then you make the optimal choice from among the group of choices that you have deduced through the process of attention and concentration. Then you make the decision and carry out the implementation, which requires the application of the mind and body to perform well in this. Work: You used all the stages and actions that slow thinking does with every situation you face, whether in life in general or in training and competing in football, which forced you to exert great mental effort. In this example that we presented, it shows us the quality of the players who execute direct free kicks in terms of the type of thinking used in the performance. After this analysis, you can determine what type of thinking is used by your colleague who executes direct free kicks in the team or even the competing players in the team. The other teams are responsible for implementing them, but this requires you to watch several videos of them executing direct free kicks.

Where you find the player who uses quick thinking is accustomed to executing free kicks in one or two specific ways all the time,which does not change his performance, which makes you easily conclude that he has practiced these two images repeatedly during training and that

he is good at them well, as he no longer uses directed attention, analysis, or the best choice. Among the solutions that he may deduce through slow thinking, based on which he makes the appropriate decision with the entire situation in terms of distance, the position of the human wall and the goalkeeper, speed, force, direction, and height required to hit the ball when executed.

As for the player who uses slow thinking, you will find, by watching his videos when executing direct free kicks, that he always renews his execution of free kicks according to the position of each kick, as we mentioned, in terms of the human wall and the position of the goalkeeper...etc.

This point is one of many points that clarify that this book was not written for a specific group, but rather includes coaches, goalkeepers, defenders, attackers, and everyone who wants to develop their technical abilities in football.

Third example

In any moment of the match in which the level of performance in terms of speed is higher than usual, in this case you need to pay attention and focus in a stronger way than usual in training and matches in which the level of performance is lower, and this naturally

requires you to exert greater mental effort, so you find… Recently, there has been a very increasing interest in the world of football training in physical preparation because of its effective impact on the technical and tactical condition of the players. On the one hand, the most important aspect is that strong physical preparation saves the players from wasting great mental effort during matches through the players' ability to Performing at speeds and abilities commensurate with any of the different playing conditions. If the players' abilities are

superior in terms of speed, for example, this forces the team's players to exert greater mental effort in the event that the opposing team

plays at a speed higher than the team is accustomed to

Characteristics of slow thinking

The previous concepts highlighted for us some important points that may make us able to understand, study and analyze slow thinking in a good way that makes us more benefit. These points are that slow thinking has a set of specific characteristics that explain its capabilities and the tasks it can perform, which makes us more interested in studying them carefully so that we can apply it. In the sports field, in ways that allow us to develop our slow thinking abilities, which helps us to advance the mental aspects that we especially neglected during the preparation and training processes due to our exaggerated interest in the physical and tactical aspects compared to the mental and psychological aspects, which are the cornerstone through which we can reach our goal. The training process.

Therefore, let us discuss the characteristics and functions of slow thinking through study and analysis in order to understand

what we do, how and why, and can we develop ?

Slow thinking is characterized by its limited concentration, and it is not at its bestin activities that exceed its ability to concentrate. In fact,

I have not found anything better than the Invisible Gorilla Experiment to illustrate this point. The Invisible Gorilla Experiment is by the scientist Christopher Sharps, a professor of psychology and executive director of the Neuroscience Program at Union University in Schenectady and scientist Daniel Simmons, a professor of psychology at the University of Illinois, and the phrase "invisible gorilla" comes from the experiment they conducted to test selective attention and focus. The experiment took place as follows A group of people attended to be a sample for the study, then one of the study leaders asked the participants to watch a video clip, where in the video there are two teams having a basketball match, one team wearing black shirts and the other wearing white shirts, and the study participants are asked to count the number of times the players pass. Those wearing white shirts throw the ball to each other. In the middle of the video, a gorilla walks during the game, stands in the middle, hits its chest, and then exits. Then the person conducting the study asks the participants

Have you seen the gorilla ????????

The strange thing is that in more than half of the cases, people completely missed seeing the gorilla, and even more so, even after telling the participants about the gorilla, they were confident that they had not missed it.The results of the study indicate that when we focus on something intently, such as driving a car on a crowded road or playing a game on the phone, we fail to discover something that enters our field of vision unexpectedly, even if it is clear and obvious. Looking at that experience, we find that directing attention and concentration is an illusion.

The most important characteristics of slow thinking: If it exceeds its capabilities, the results will be unexpected.

In fact, the study of hidden gorillas not only provides an example of the limited focus of slow thinking, but also that it is often an illusion. The gorilla

experiment shows us the illusion of attention, which says that we believe that we pay attention to the world around us much more than we actually do. In the experiment, the participants focus on counting the number of passes, and this represents a specific task, and that focusing on this task made them lose sight of the gorilla that appeared clearly in the video. Whereas at first the people who had not seen the gorilla insisted that such an animal not appear in the video clip, they did not imagine in any caseIt is possible for them to miss something like this. Some even accused those conducting the study of showing a different video the second

time.This shows that slow thinking has limited focus for us when we face activities that require attention and intense concentration, as we are unable to pay attention and be aware of all the events that are happening around us while immersed in the video. These activities, therefore, often expose us to what is called the illusion of attention.

(Illustrative examples through football)

First example

When the coach's instructions before a match against a strong team are clear that it is necessary to shoot at the goal at any opportunity that allows the players to do so, in this case what is called the phenomenon of directed attention occurs among the players, which often forces our minds to ignore some details and events in order to focus on The main event, which here is to shoot at the opposing team's goal as soon as the playing conditions allow for doing so. I believe that after the end of the match,

regardless of the result, if the coach replays the match summary to the players through the video, there will be surprising scenes during the video that indicate mishandling.

Players with a lot of playing situations that if they had been exploited better instead of directly shooting at the goal, the goals would have been achieved. This shows us one of the images that may make the focus of our slow thinking limited and unable to be aware of many of the playing situations that happen around us during the course of

the match. If we can direct our attention better, we will be able to exploit many opportunities better.

Second example

When the tactical aspect of a team is based on preparing the attack from the back line, and this is practiced over and over again during daily training sessions, this makes the focus of the players in the back line largely directed towards the task of the necessity of preparing from the back line, which may often make them oblivious to situations. Better for passing, it may save them the misery of preparing from the back line, so we explain here that coaches must be flexible, when developing the tactical aspect, so that they give the players the

freedom to do what is appropriate for the playing situation they are dealing with during their possession of the ball, and that the coaches must encourage the players to do so and He presents to them the idea of the necessity of thinking

outside the box while playing and not necessarily adhering to game plans all the time, as this frees their slow thinking from the idea of the task and the attention directed to it, which makes them more attentive to the different playing situations and the movements of their colleagues.

And competitors and good awareness free of restrictions, which makes them more agile and intelligent in dealing with different playing situations.

Slow thinking cannot perform several activities at the same time

Slow thinking is characterized by its inability to perform more than one activity that requires the exertion of great mental effort at one time, as it requires directing attention and focus towards one activity. If it does the opposite, things will not be in their correct position, as we previously explained that slow thinking has limited focus. When dealing with a single situation that requires intense attention and concentration, it makes us overlook many events that are clear and evident. The best example is what was mentioned about the experience of the hidden gorilla.

Example for clarification

If you are walking you can think at the same time about your plan for tomorrow so your mind is doing two things at the same time in fact it is doing a lot of things at the same time but it is not focused on walking it is almost automatic. On the other hand, a oneyear-old One while he is learning to walk, he is completely focused on it and cannot do other things at the same time. When he tries to do that, he usually falls, and returning to walking, if you need to focus on something very important, such as giving instructions to someone on how to land a plane, you will stop walking as To use your full focus on the most important task at hand. Note that walking does not generally require concentration, but it does use some of your brain power. If you try to focus on two tasks at the same time, such as watching an exciting premiere movie while writing an important report, you will end up jumping back and forth between Both tasks, but you will not focus on both at the same time, so you will find that there are common factors between fast and slow thinking, as you use both at the same time sometimes, and you use slow thinking sometimes, and other times when the matter is more complex and requires intense concentration and greater mental effort, but you cannot Using that thinking to perform more than one task requires concentration, strength, and mental effort, as we explained

(Some illustrative examples through football) First example

One of the important things that we would like to clarify at this point is that often when coaches make plans and the tactical aspect of the team, we often find some players having multiple tasks and a tactical complex on the field, and sometimes we find that some players succeed in this and other times they fail, and here the matter is not related to the aspect. Physically or the players' lack of understanding of the roles that the coach gives them. Rather, the matter lies in the fact that sometimes when the player is assigned more than one task on the field, the playing conditions and situations are different and superior to the player's technical and tactical abilities, which forces the player to raise levels of concentration and thus distracts the player's attention between the roles assigned to him. In it, he is required to make a greater mental effort in order to pay attention and focus in all playing situations. Here we explain to the coaches who do this work the necessity of a good study of the complex roles that are given to the players and to reconsider them with each match and analyze them well to see whether they are compatible with the player's fast and slow thinking capabilities. Or will it be more focused on slow thinking, which forces the player to exert greater mental effort, causing him distraction and many mistakes, as it is necessary for the coach to understand the player's mental capabilities before

the physical, technical, and tactical abilities, because in the end the mental aspect is primarily responsible for implementing all matters. Other aspects are in the required forms, and therefore the coach must have a good vision of the player's mental capabilities in terms of the player's balance and strength of quick thinking and the skills, beliefs, and tools of slow thinking.

Second example

When the attacking player on the team is alone with the opposing team's goalkeeper, the first thing that makes him make a mistake in scoring a goal is for the player to think about two things, such as: Should I dodge the goalkeeper or do I shoot directly? In this case, you have made the mind think between two things in a playing situation that cannot be tolerated any longer. For a second or two at most, you delegated the matter to slow thinking, and you also introduced two thoughts into it, both of which require attention and concentration in order to make an appropriate decision, and this is not compatible with the capabilities of slow thinking, which results in the failure of the attack and the loss of the opportunity before the attacker, as it is very necessary to Players know the characteristics of both fast thinking and slow thinking, on the basis of which players can choose the best decisions that suit both types of thinking.

You pay attention to that sound from any direction, and quick thinking begins to provide quick suggestions, as the sound distinguishes whether it is panic, happiness, or anger, but then when you see the source of the sound, you can assess the situation well.

You choose the best suggestion from among the suggestions offered by fast thinking. You can also ignore that sound or not. This represents the ability of slow thinking to control your attention whether you want to continue paying attention or not.

Slow thinking is characterized by laziness:

If I asked you to solve a problem such as the product of 29*41 = ...

If you have not tried to solve the problem before and do not know the result at first glance, the first thing you will think about is using the calculator on your phone because you know that the matter will be exhausting and require more mental effort to solve the problem

if you do not rely on the calculator, and this It explains to us that when we are exposed to new information, knowledge, or skills, the first

thing the mind thinks about is escaping the use of slow thinking by relying on quick thinking suggestions.

Example for clarification

When you decide to take a trip by car to a city, and you know that it has two roads, you can take one of them in order to reach it. The first road is short but crowded and requires residential areas around it. The second road is long but not

crowded and not populated, which makes driving better. The faster you will most likely choose the long route.

(Illustrative examples through football) First example

When a team needs to attack in order to score a goal against a team that is defensively strong and well organized, in such a situation the team needs players who have deep thoughts in passing to solve defensive blocks, and doing so requires the player to do more visual scanning. Understanding the defensive movements of competitors, as well as evaluating the movements of teammates and choosing the best among them for passing, as well as linking the speed and strength required to pass the ball and the distance between him and the receiver. In fact, you will not find many players doing this, as at the maximum you will find two to three players in each team.

Whoever has the ability to overcome the laziness of their slow thinking, while the rest of the players will have traditional and superficial passes for most of the game time. A large part of this is due to their inability to overcome the nature of their laziness and slow thinking. Many times in different playing situations you find behavior Some players with the ball are very superficial and the passes they make are very legible and easy

Therefore, it is necessary for the coach to pay attention to planning exercises that encourage players to pay attention, exert mental effort, and think well during training.

Through everything mentioned above in this chapter, we can realize well that the two basic factors influencing our slow thinking performance are (attention - and mental effort).

Chapter III

The relationship between fast and slow thinking

Fast and slow thinking are in an active state the entire time we stay awake, Fast thinking always works automatically, as we mentioned previously, and slow thinking works with low effort, as it uses little of its ability. Fast thinking all the time makes suggestions to slow thinking. Slow thinking takes those suggestions with input. Some modifications to them or without modifications at all, as we often believe in the way our minds work, which works according to what we believe, and that this belief comes from the impression that arises with the situations that we encounter during life, so we do not need to modify these suggestions all the time, as they represent... Our impression of the situations and things we experience in life is considered one of the characteristics of quick thinking, as we explained previously, This

shows us the effect of the impression that draws us towards something, as it often directs us to a way of thinking that is appropriate for that impression, and as we mentioned previously, it is often... Those impressions are wrong, and this is what calls for us to reconsider our impression and reshape it somewhat so that we can think in more logical ways that make us make decisions and judge things with a logical argument and not our prevailing impression. The work is between them, but when quick thinking faces difficulty and is unable to provide a solution to it, Slow thinking intervenes to address the problem and provide the appropriate solution to it.

Indeed, for example, when you are possessed by the ball in the middle of the field and do not find any of your teammates in a suitable position to pass the ball to, in this case slow thinking intervenes, as you begin to pay conscious attention and focus and analyze the situation and search for... Memory about a situation similar to that situation until you reach an appropriate solution for that situation. Therefore, we can say that quick thinking works all the time as long as he does not encounter a problem for which he cannot provide a suggestion or that something wrong is about to happen. Otherwise, quick thinking does its job efficiently. High all the time, as it is characterized by speed and continuous suggestions

for the normal situations that we go through throughout the day. For example, during the course of play in a match, many of your decisions are quick and do not require mental effort or low effort and you do not need to think. Fast thinking, except when the playing situations are difficult and complex and quick thinking cannot provide appropriate suggestions, in this case slow thinking intervenes to take over. As for the shortcomings that make us anxious about the suggestions he presents, they are illogical and unstoppable, as we

mentioned previously, and here an analogy can be made. Fast thinking with good soil that accepts all seeds, good and bad, fruitful and unfruitful roses and thorns. Since fast thinking is like this,

then we must choose the good seeds (ideas) that produce good beliefs and sound ideas for us within our fast thinking, and from here we must change the reason, which is the method. In which we use our slow thinking until the result changes, which represents the impressions, feelings, and ideas that fast thinking has as a result of the work that slow

thinking does with every new knowledge or situation we are exposed to during life, as fast thinking responds to those ideas that slow thinking deposits with it. Every situation, for example if you are responsible for implementing

Direct free kicks in the team, and the rate of translating those kicks into goals for you ranges between 1:2 out of 10, and this is a weak rate compared to the upper levels of first-class players. This is despite the fact that your technical and physical capabilities are good. Here we can say that the problem lies in the training process. Even if you train on this over and over again, the problem is qualitative and not quantitative, meaning that the way in which the training is done and the quality of the exercises is not appropriate, as fast thinking

represents the random memory of the mind, and if not slow thinking is able to deposit the information, knowledge and techniques related

to correct direct free kicks into that. Memory, implementation during matches will not be as hoped, as we have previously said that when you plant thorns, you do not wait to reap roses

For example

but not limited to, the information and knowledge required for this is the player's knowledge of the speed of the ball and the mechanical properties of that speed, whether on the ground or in the air, and the relationship between those. Speed, distance traveled, time, and the speed of the goalkeeper's reaction according to the place he is on the goal line, the legal distance to the human wall made up of the opposing team's defenders, the number of these defenders, and the relationship of that to the goalkeeper's field of vision and its effect on his reaction, and the strength of the striking man from stability and approach, and the relationship of the distance of the approach to strength. The kick, as well as the angle of the body, starting from the head to the toenails of the foot, and its relationship to the direction of the ball and its rotation, whether on the ground or in the air, and this is affected by the weather conditions, such as wind and rain. In the end, the training method that is matched by slow thinking must be well

suited to his ability, allowing it to be stored. In the memory with good images so that quick thinking can retrieve them in an accurate and correct way. In the end, we can say that fast thinking is a reflection of the information, knowledge, and beliefs that slow thinking provides to it. It is clear from the previous example that quick thinking had the upper hand in deciding the outcome of training, exercises, and methods.

If the training is good, the execution of the kicks will be better, and if it is not good, the execution will not be as desired.

Therefore, slow and fast thinking are like two work groups working within one system by connecting to a wireless device, where the first group, which represents slow thinking, works inside the control and monitoring room.

Therefore, it is responsible for sending work information to the second group, which represents fast thinking, which takes the information and implements it as It is without interference from them, as any error in implementation may cause a problem, and this is from the vision of the first group. The mission of that group is to operate the machines and do everything necessary according to the information issued by the first group, and this shows that slow thinking is the leader of your ideas and the one responsible for issuing them or not. Fast thinking is responsible for maintaining and believing in those ideas and acting on them as they are.

Another example to clarify

Slow thinking is like the navigator and captain of a ship standing at the bow. He directs the ship and issues orders to the ship's crew in the engine room, who control the boilers and who measure the distances between the ship and other ships. The men in the engine room do

not know where they are heading (quick thinking), so they follow orders. The ship may collide with rocks if the captain of the ship standing

at the bow issues incorrect instructions based on the results of the work of other devices, such as the compass and the celestial body measuring instrument.

The workers in the engine room obey the ship captain because he is responsible and issues orders that are implemented automatically. Members of the ship's crew do not review the commander's instructions. Because he is supposed to be confident in what he is doing, they simply carry out his instructions, as fast thinking receives information from slow thinking and believes in it as it is and does not question it or the basis of its source and its validity or not.

For example, when you say and repeat that you will fail to take a penalty kick, quick thinking takes and stores that information, causing you to lack and fear failure when taking penalty kicks. In fact, you are the one who caused that problem, as it could have been successfully overcome had it not been for you. The negative thoughts that I leaked into quick thinking without need for that, instead of negative thoughts, it would have been better, for example, to watch the best players who take penalty kicks and say that if I can take penalty kicks like those players, I am not missing anything from them, but rather I have them. The same capabilities are nothing but a training problem, and I only have to train like them so that I can develop my skill in executing penalty kicks in a wonderful way. Positive thoughts like these help you

reach positive results.

Another example to clarify

When you are playing as a center back in a big match, and before the match, the coach assigns you to monitor the opposing team's striker, who is a very distinguished striker, as he is ranked the best striker in the league, and you possess all the resistances of a good defender, and before the match, the coach motivates you that you can control that striker, as you have Good skills to do this work, and you also repeated positive thoughts inside yourself, such as "I can," which is not a difficult thing, but rather a pleasure when you face a

challenge like this. In fact, those thoughts will creep into your quick thinking, and if you are in good physical, technical, and tactical

condition, most likely you will succeed. In stopping that attacker with ease and without mental and psychological trouble, since you have prepared yourself mentally and psychologically very well, it will help you do your job with high efficiency, but that depends on your belief in what you say and not just verbal implementation, but that motivation and positive thoughts must reach your thinking. The quick one and leave it to him after that, as he is good at implementing what you believe in well

Another example

We often see some distinguished players fail to score penalty kicks, especially in big and decisive matches. This is often due to the leakage of fear, anxiety, and expressions of failure from their slow thinking to their quick thinking, whether that leakage occurred before the match or during the match as a result of crowd pressure and the atmosphere of the match in general. In the end, we find that these players take penalty kicks in such matches in a way that is strange and inferior to matches that are under less psychological and public pressure.

You find them aiming the ball either with an exaggerated force that results in the ball risinghigher than the kicker, or exaggerating in directing the ball to the right or left. This results in the ball going away from the goal post, or they change the way they execute the penalty kick, which often results in reckless execution.

Another example to clarify

The same applies to training in basic skills. For the mind, they represent a set of information and knowledge that translates into practical performance represented by basic skills. If the exercises and exercises are not prepared in a way that is compatible with the capabilities and characteristics of slow thinking in the required manner, the results that quick thinking will provide will not be satisfactory. During competitions, we have previously explained that the relationship between slow and fast thinking is a cause-and-effect relationship, and that the better the cause, the better the result, and vice versa. For example, when planning basic skills development exercises, it is necessary to take into account the characteristics and factors affecting slow thinking, such as attention and the degree of mental effort that It is required to perform the exercise.

Taking into

account these points is very important, as it helps players develop the two functions of the mind: fast thinking and slow thinking in a good Way, players' A model exercise that takes into account the development of slow thinking abilities.

Exercise name : Shaded rectangle

Objective of the exercise : Developing players' divided attention - developing foot passing

Tools and equipment : stadium29 * 29 m – Footballs – Gear for field planning – Whistle

Organization and preparation : The coach plans the field into two equal squares separated by a shaded rectangle three meters wide

Each square has four players wearing uniforms numbered from one to four, and a defender with a different uniform. Each player has possession of the ball.

Instructions : The players of each square exchange balls with each other, with

the players of each square trying to deceive the other square This is as follows: If a player enters the shaded rectangle separating the two squares, it is necessary to exchange passes with him. The player wearing the same shirt number is in the other square. The player who does not notice this within three seconds switches roles with the defender in his own square.

Technical points : The coach focuses on the level of attention and speed of the players, as well as the correct performance of passing with the sole of the foot.

We notice in this exercise that it takes into account the mental capabilities of the players and seeks to develop them in a practical and tangible way, as it sees the capabilities of slow thinking through the players' attention to the skill of passing with the sole of the foot correctly, while paying attention to other stimuli, such as the movement of one of the players towards the shaded rectangle. This is what is imposed on the players. Exerting great mental effort at the same time takes into account the capabilities of quick thinking through the necessity of speed in passing . account the capabilities and characteristics of fast and slow thinking, and we did not delve into the complex exercises that contain more than one characteristic of fast and slow thinking together, is that such exercises will help us build and develop our mental abilities in line with training techniques and plans. And football competitions, which helps to raise the skill level of players in a practical and tangible way through their understanding of the nature of the human mind, its functions, and the characteristics of each job, and translating that into exercises, drills, and real training plans in which the mental aspect is taken into account as much as the physical and tactical aspects are taken into account.

Just as this helps to develop the players' abilities, it also It aims to develop the capabilities of coaches and opens horizons for them to strive to

build new exercises, drills and game plans. It also helps them to choose new methods of training that contribute to the realization of their new training ideas, including It is consistent with training methods that seek to take into account the mental aspect of players, and from here we have built a complete methodology for exercises that aim to achieve these goals. When you think with your conscious mind, which represents slow thinking, repeatedly or habitually, these thoughts are immersed within your fast thinking, which represents The beating heart of emotions, emotions, and feelings, as we mentioned previously.

Therefore, when you train through such exercises in a way that takes into account the characteristics of the two functions of the mind in a normal way, you give quick thinking the opportunity to be creative and bring and propose more ideas and decisions that carry a large aspect of rationality, logic, and wise and creative behavior with every situation. Of the various playing situations, whether at the level of training or competition, and as we know and we mentioned this, one of the characteristics of quick thinking is that it deals with new ideas in a literal manner that does not differentiate between reward and error, as it depends on the belief and belief of the thinking, and therefore if those ideas are wrong and they represent a cause, then the result You will be up to that reason and that is why we call on trainers to choose ideas that are in line with the capabilities of the mind and take into account its various characteristics, as we find many trainers building exercises according to physical,

skill and tactical performance without looking at mental performance even though it is the dynamo and the main engine through which To improve all other aspects, the trainer must take this into account and move away from the idea of indoctrination or training that restricts the mind and its properties, as this approach is similar to dealing with a machine or a computer. We give it orders according to specific steps and it implements according to those orders. This principle is very different from the principles of dealing with... The human mind has a complex nature and intertwined characteristics. This is one aspect. The other aspect is that this human mind during matches deals with different situations, as it is difficult to form specific commands for all football situations, but it is correct to prepare that mind to deal according to its functions and characteristics to manage different situations in ways that suit each. A situation in the game, as we can program the mind for this matter, on the contrary, we cannot program the different situations, which are sometimes new and complex at other times.

Example for clarification

Throughout your training life and the local and international competitions that you participate in, and together with each of the matches that you participate in, you often encounter new playing situations that you may not have been exposed to during your entire training life, and this happens repeatedly during matches for all players, but your ability to act in such The different situations of playing are the ones that explain the extent of your use of mental abilities, the two functions of fast and slow thinking, and the characteristics of each of them. Here, we must clarify the difference between innate talent and acquired talent so that you can know the value and importance of developing mental abilities in football. We have heard a lot about the term innate talent in sports, which means that it is not acquired, as the individual is born with it. God has given him those abilities without human intervention, and when we mention that term in football, the first players who... They come to our mind: the Brazilian Ronaldinho, the Brazilian Pele, the Argentinian Messi, and the Argentine Maradona. These are examples, but not limited to them. What is important about the topic is that when you watch these players on television playing matches, you find that they are performing the basic and individual skills with ease and pleasant simplicity. When one of them possesses the ball, you expect no danger. It is impossible and everything that is difficult for them is very easy.

Do you know why? Because they simply realize what they are doing in every situation they face, and this awareness comes from their brilliant abilities in using their mental abilities and their good exploitation of their fast and slow thinking abilities. For example, you find them making charming passes that make you say how he was able to analyze the movements of his teammates and competitors and estimate the distance in order to make that pass. Since you answered the question yourself, where he paid attention, focused, analyzed, selected, and made the appropriate decision, and these represent the two functions of the mind, fast and slow thinking, so these players' talent lies in making good use of their mental abilities before making good use of their skill abilities.

As for the other aspect of talent, it is acquired talent, which means that there is a specific aspect of innate talent that the player and coach were able to develop to reach the maximum levels of efficiency during performance, and when we mention that type of skill, we must mention the Portuguese star Cristiano Ronaldo and the star Mohamed Salah.

In short, these players have a certain part of the skill that they were able to reach the top through training, and here we stop to ask the question: What training did these players receive to reach that skill? In fact, the issue here stops at two points that explain the quality of training

First point

These players were interested in developing their mental abilities in terms of attention, concentration, good choice, good analysis of playing situations, good behavior, and quick decision-making. In fact, you can do this without a coach if you have sufficient will, as it depends only on your understanding of the nature of your mind's work, its functions, and the characteristics of each function. On the one hand, this is your belief in the importance of developing these abilities and that they are no less important than physical, skill, and tactical abilities.

The second point

The second point is the way in which exercises and exercises are dealt with, as these players look at exercises in a way that helps them exploit them in a way that is consistent with developing their mental abilities, which often helps them to Achieving their goals during matches, or in other words, they see and deal with exercises in a way that serves their abilities, whether mental, skill, physical or tactical, at the same level, as they do not preoccupy themselves with the skill or the physical aspect rather than the mental aspect.

This shows us the importance of exploiting our mental abilities and developing them during training and competitions.

Many times we find that some players do not have any mental vision while dealing with different playing situations, but rather their total dependence on the physical, skill and tactical aspects is unconscious, which often wastes this expended energy. In these aspects, there is no significant benefit. For example, we often encounter some players with wonderful skills, but they were not good at exploiting them, and the cost of this was the loss of their football future. This is often due to those players not paying attention to the necessity of linking their good skills, which are represented by basic and individual skills. Finding it and mastering its performance in a wonderful, automated way, and their mental skills of attention and concentration and the ability to choose the suggestions presented by quick thinking between different playing situations and the good implementation of decisions, and this is similar to birds that fly in names, as they are good at flying but do not know the laws of mechanics that explain and explain this process of flying, on the contrary. Man, before the invention of the airplane, could not fly in the air, but when he wanted to, he began to think and look around him. This is what led the famous Arab scientist Abbas Ibn Firnas, who carried out the first experiment in flight, taking advantage of the environment around him.

He looked at the bird and contemplated and began to prepare for his idea and applied it practically. Why did the world pay attention to this issue for research and experimentation until we reached where we are now of tremendous progress? Man was able to reach the moon and cross the world by air. In the end, man was able to move forward as he used his mental abilities to achieve what he wanted and he was able to do that through research and experimentation. As for the birds that owned the atmosphere before man thought and directed his attention to the necessity of moving through the air, for millions of years, they were not able to understand a single law of mechanics that explains the bird and how it happens. This is natural because they do not have the mind with which God distinguished man over all other creatures, but what is surprising is that To find 22 players in a match, some of them know the meaning of the mind, how it works, the characteristics of its functions, and the characteristics of each function, which makes them, in many different playing situations, resemble a bird that does not understand any of the laws of mechanics that explain how the process of flight occurs, and this is what we call on players and coaches to pay attention to. The mental aspect in a practical and tangible way, far from words and constructive ideas that we cannot apply practically in the field of teaching and competition so that we can improve our mental abilities during performance

and competition in accordance with the latest developments in football and the tremendous progress that has occurred in the physical, tactical and skill aspects so that we can advance the game more. Popular all over the world, the bottom line in the nature of the relationship between fast and slow thinking with regard to ideas is that you will get a response or reaction from fast thinking according to the nature of the idea that you retain and believe in slow thinking, and numerous studies conducted by scientists and doctors have

proven that fast thinking is not Able to choose and compare, which is necessary for the process of logical thinking, as these studies have shown that quick thinking accepts any assumptions, regardless of whether they are true or false.

It accepts and responds according to what slow thinking assumes and approves, while fast thinking works to link old ideas with new ones in order to achieve the goal you want.

How do both slow and fast thinking derive their working tools? First, slow thinking

Slow thinking obtains perception from the environment through observation and is used to do so The five senses are understood through observation, experience, and education through many different life experiences and situations.

For example

you cannot know that one of the players on the team possesses multiple and wonderful individual skills except through your observation of him during training and matches, during which you learn about his abilities and can judge what he has. Whether these abilities are really

amazing or are they ordinary and not striking

Another example to clarify

When you use slow thinking to make a long pass to an attacker, for example, you need to do a visual scan first, and here you have used the sense of sight in order to be able to obtain sufficient information about the playing situation.

Then, you analyze which of the attackers is most appropriate to pass to, and then you make a decision. Appropriately, in this situation, you needed the sense of sight in order for slow thinking to perform the task, as the senses are considered one of the important tools from which slow thinking begins, and therefore attention, whether auditory or visual, has a major role in determining our slow thinking capabilities.

Secondly, quick thinking

Quick thinking works through intuition, which is the basis of emotions and feelings And feelings and works with different tools, far from the five senses, as quick thinking sees without the need for the sense of sight. He can see everything that is located beyond the range of sight, which is called clairvoyance or sharpness of perception. Many times, during a fast performance in football, you find yourself performing A pass, whether short or long, without looking at your colleague's position, but with acute awareness and foresight, you are aware and know that he will be in the place where you passed the ball in that situation of play. Such a situation often

happens with us, but we do not realize or search for the reason for its occurrence, and this is what makes us unable to pass it. Accessing the creative abilities of quick thinking, and this shows us that it is not necessary to think fast in order to perform its various tasks because it depends on intuition, emotions, feelings and experiences stored in memory that help it perform many activities during different playing situations without the need to use the senses.

Another example to clarify

During public matches and the stadium is full of fans, you cannot hear the voice of your teammates. If you make a bad pass to one of your teammates and he cannot reach it, without him speaking or pointing to you with his hand, you can understand what he wants to say, not because you have the seventh sense, but because you have... The most important abilities are the abilities of quick thinking, which relies on tools that make you anticipate and perform some activities during gaming situations without the need for the senses.

the fourth chapter

Developing slow thinking abilities for football players (a) Attention

Develop slow thinking abilities for football players

Through our study of slow thinking, we learned about its concept, its characteristics, the functions it performs, and how it performs them. Through that study, it becomes clear to us that the two basic factors in the work of slow thinking and those responsible for its creation or failure are (attention - mental effort).

Therefore, it was necessary to direct attention to these two factors to a good extent and look at the most important studies that would explain to us the concept, characteristics, nature, influencing factors, and how to develop and treat each of these two factors because of their great importance with regard to one of the functions of the mind, which is slow thinking, which is

considered a stone. The corner for developing the second function of the mind, which is rapid thinking. This is at the level of daily life in general. In many situations that we are exposed to during the day, we need to use our slow thinking abilities. For example, but not limited to, when you buy something, whether it is clothes, gifts, or... Anything whose price has fractions, such as 12523.

If you are not good at mathematical operations, you will focus your attention on knowing what the price will be if you buy three of the same kind, and this will also consume a lot of your energy and mental effort, as well as when you study a new lesson that

contains information and knowledge. New, this also requires slow thinking abilities. Likewise, in football, many, many playing

situations during matches require slow thinking abilities, including, for example, executing direct free kicks, penalty kicks, and

other dynamic playing situations, and this is what we will explain in what follows. Through some examples and models that show

us the importance of developing our slow thinking abilities. Therefore, in this chapter we will discuss

Attention - its concept - its types - the factors affecting each type - and how to plan football training according to the characteristics and capabilities of each type of attention.

First, attention

The study of attention is a major part of contemporary psychology and neuroscience, as attention plays a crucial role in perception, which affects the decisions we make. Therefore, the study of attention is of interest to many psychologists, and among the issues that have been addressed, which represents the focus of our study of attention, is The role of attention in awareness and conscious thought and whether

attention is voluntarily or involuntarily directed towards things and events. This is what prompts us to study the nature of the relationship between attention and conscious thought, which represents slow thinking, so that we can stand on some points that may help us in building a good methodology for developing attention in people. Football players during training and competition, which helps them use slow thinking more effectively, as attention represents the first step in the learning process. Everyone may fail to pay attention sometimes, but some people fail to pay attention often, which causes them many problems, whether during training. Or the competition and what the player may be affected by as a result of his continuous failure to pay attention to important stimuli and information during matches, which

affects many of his technical decisions during performance, as it is easy for almost anyone to pay attention to the stimuli and information that interests him,

and at the same time it is difficult for people to They pay attention to stimuli, information, and things that do not interest them. For example, we may pay attention to the television while sitting at home because we are temporarily happy. Therefore, at the same time, while paying attention to the television that caught our attention, we may overlook another stimulus or stimulus that may be no less important or may be more important. Such as not paying attention to the phone ring or the door of the house. This is what makes us more anxious about paying attention to some things and not paying attention to others. This explains that we are only aware of what we pay attention to. As for what we miss, we are oblivious to it and do not know anything about it at the time it happens, which is in the future. The same place they are in. For example, the attacker who has possession of the ball may make a pass to one of his teammates. At the same time, there may be another teammate who is better in position and movement, but he has neglected to pay attention to him for some reason, which makes the attacker, after the end of the match and reviewing the video, be He was very surprised and wondered how I had

overlooked that situation and did not see it even though it was on the field of play that I was on the field. People also differ in their ability to focus their attention at the right time on what is right. In the same previous example, if the striker is replaced by another striker.

He is distinguished by his ability to focus his attention at the right time in a correct manner. His passing decisions will often be better, and this is natural given that we are hidden from each other in terms of abilities, skills, talent and special techniques on the field, where there are

always individual differences between each other, but in At the same time, we know that we can develop many of the abilities, techniques, and skills that we possess, and this shows us the importance of studying attention to learn about its abilities, properties, types, and the most important theories in psychology that have studied and analyzed it so that we are more aware of our ability.

We must pay attention to what degree we can develop his abilities in order to reach our primary goal, which is to develop our ability to think slowly during training and competition.

The concept of attention

We use the word "attention" all the time, but what processes or abilities does this term refer to? We use the word

"attention" a lot on the roads, during transportation, and in buildings to warn against smoking...etc. Let us discuss some of the concepts of attention that were discussed. Psychologists are studying this so we can better understand this term

The concept of attention

It is the ability to effectively process specific information in the environment while controlling other details. Attention is limited in capacity and duration, so it is important that we have ways to effectively manage the attentional resources available to us.

Another concept to pay attention to

The psychologist and philosopher (William James) wrote in his book "Principles of Psychology" that attention is "the clear and vivid possession of the mind by one of what may seem to be several possible things or trains of thought at the same time." It means withdrawing from some things in order to deal effectively with them. With other things.

Through these concepts, we can say for clarification that attention is a tool for discrimination. For example, during a performance in a match, you make a long pass to your attacking teammate. In this case, the important part of the field is highlighted in order to do this, which is the place where your attacking teammate is located. It is not just a matter of your focusing on the area in which your colleague is located, but rather it involves you ignoring a large amount of the playing field and the amount of information and other stimuli it contains that compete with the area in which your colleague is located. This shows that attention is ignoring information and perceptions that are not relevant at the time. This is in order to focus on important information, and it also affects our perception of the stimuli surrounding us-

Another example to clarify: - When you shoot a penalty kick, it is necessary that you direct attention to your decision to shoot and the goal kick only,

and that at this moment you ignore any other information or incentives that are not related to shooting the penalty kick, as you ignore anything else that might... It affects the task to which attention is directed, whether intentionally or unintentionally.

Here we must clarify the relationship between attention and perception and the difference between them so that we do not get confused between the work of each of

them

Attention is what enables a person to choose his field of interest. For example, the ability to have a phone conversation in the middle of a concert, or to listen to your friend in the middle of a concert, or to pay attention to someone you know in the middle of a large crowd of people, or to monitor the movements of your colleague on the field in order to choose the appropriate time to pass to him, are all examples that show that attention is what enables us to choose.

The field of attention that we want. As for perception, it is the ability for a person to perceive his environment through creating meaning from what our five sensory organs obtain, as it allows us to interpret the information and expectations that exist. Therefore, perception enables us to create meaning from the sensory nerves,

and for this reason we can say that the five senses are It determines how we perceive things. For example, when we see the light of a car coming on the road, we are unconsciously able to interpret what this light means. Likewise, when we hear certain sounds, we can interpret them and form an image based on them. This clarifies the relationship between attention and perception. For example, when we hear the sound of barking. With a dog, our brain is able to process information and create an image even though we do not see the dog at that moment, as perception is determined by the culture and experiences that the individual has had before, and before someone can choose the place or anything to focus on, he uses one of the two methods.

The first method : - "From the bottom up" and allows the individual to scan the environment or his mind in search of existing information

The second method : - "From top to bottom" depends on the individual's goals, which can lead to the formation of a habit. For example, if the attacker in the team gets used to shooting (R2), he will tend to focus his attention while in possession of the ball on the appropriate places in front of the opposing team's penalty area to implement it. That skill.

The bottom line is that attention and perception depend on each other, as perception interprets what we see and hear in images that we can understand before the mind takes any action. Attention captures the image and determines what we will focus on based on our experiences, goals, and areas of interest, and this relationship between attention and focus is what determines our ability to Discovering the stimuli that occur around us correctly and appropriately during matches. Therefore, the relationship between attention and perception is interconnected in the presence of the stimulus or stimulus. Studies have proven that when we perceive something we have to pay attention to it. For example, when you perceive the opponent's movement in front of your team's goal in A gaming situation. You naturally direct your attention to this player in order to make the appropriate decision in order to control him and thwart his attempts.

When we focus attention on something, we are able to perceive more details. In

the same previous example, after focusing your attention on the player's movements, you discover more. The goal of that move that the player makes, and this shows us how important it is

Developing the process of perception alongside developing attention because they are two interconnected and complementary processes in the end, both of which help the other complete its task with quality and efficiency.

Types of attention

When talking about attention, we must know what the types and role of each type are and the characteristics that distinguish it from others so that we can reach our main goal, which is to develop the slow thinking abilities of players during training and competition, as there are many types of attention that differ from each other according to... Our attention needs. For example, does the task we are doing require full attention, or do we need to focus on one thing while ignoring other things that are happening at the same time, or must we do two activities at the same time? This shows us that our type of attention is different.

Depending on what we need in a specific situation, and

necessarily during training and competition in football, we need different types of attention, as the football match is not at one pace or a unified position that follows the same approach throughout the match, but rather the exact opposite, as football positions are variable and not uniform. The same pace, but every second in the match has a different playing situation from the other, and each of those situations requires a certain type of attention in order to continue performing well throughout the ninety minutes.

This is what forces us to direct attention to studying the types of attention well in order to determine The truth about what attention we need during the match and how we can introduce different types of attention into exercises and training, which allows us to develop it in a consistent and correct way with the basic skills in football, allowing us to build modern exercises that are compatible with the situations and course of play during training and competition, research that allows for the development of abilities and skills. Mentality is as much as it allows for the development of basic skills, physical preparation, and planning.

Let us study the types of attention so that we can identify the characteristics and role of each type of attention.

Scientists divide attention into several types, as follows:

- Constant attention

- Selective attention - Divided attention

- Focused attention

- Alternating attention

First : - constant attention The concept of sustained attention: -

It is the process that enables the continuous performance of tasks over long periods of time. Continuous attention is one of the basic elements or components of attention processes, as it allows maintaining alertness, selective and focused attention, persistence in response, and continuous effort despite changing circumstances.

Understandably, it becomes clear to us that sustained attention is what enables us to maintain the focus of our attention on the stimulus for a long period of time, even if there is a period of fatigue or when there are distracting factors. Continuous attention is divided into alertness, which enables us to discover the stimulus when it appears, and concentration, which It allows us to focus our attention on this stimulus, and adults usually have an attention span of about 15 to 20 minutes. There are many different stimuli and they may be external or related to the game, such as the coach's instructions, the position of the ball, the movements of competitors, the movements of colleagues, the cheers of the audience, or the time of the match.

Or referee decisions and other external stimuli. There are also internal stimuli represented by our impressions, feelings and thoughts. In light of all these stimuli, you are required during the match to maintain attention to the stimuli related to

performance during the match throughout the time of the match. This is continuous attention as the concept indicates.

This type of attention, the performance it performs, whether positive or negative, affects other types of attention. For example, if our continuous attention is affected, it may lead to the deterioration of selective attention because it requires that the person have the ability to focus attention.

(Some illustrative examples of sustained attention) First example

In fact, many of the activities that we do in our daily lives require a certain level of sustained attention, whether it is watching a movie, preparing food, doing office work while working, or even taking a shower. In fact, while you are reading this book, you are

now using sustained attention.

Second example

Driving a car requires constant attention, as we must monitor the road and be well attentive, otherwise the consequences will not be good, and this shows that constant attention is with us in many of the tasks that we perform.

Third example

School students also have to pay close attention during the lesson given to them by the teacher, as well as when they study at home. This is so that the outcome of the conversation will be more beneficial, as without paying attention they will overlook many important points present in the lesson they are studying, whether at school or at home.

Fourth example

Likewise, football players during the match are always in need of continuous attention, whether at the level of alertness, which represents the basic stage of continuous attention, which is represented in the players' ability to discover new incentives that they are exposed to with

each of the different playing situations, as football is characterized by speed. And the change in terms of physical,

skill and tactical performance with each of the different playing situations, or in the level of focus of attention, or the focus that allows us to focus our

attention on this stimulus during play. For example, during play you are required to follow the position of the ball and the movements of teammates and competitors and respond to every stimulus. It comes from them and you realize whether it needs to focus on it or continue to pay attention to the playing situation in general, and so during the different playing situations the action remains in this state.

Fifth example

When you perform offensive planning work with colleagues, this work requires continuous attention in order to continue working from the beginning until the end of the attack with good efficiency and without errors. You need continuous focus on performing the task.

This explains the role and importance of continuous attention in football matches, which makes us necessarily search for ways that help us develop it in a way that makes our abilities equivalent to the playing situations during matches to a good degree,

and this work in fact requires a good and effective solution, as football is as We mentioned that it is full of many distractions that would affect the ability to provide continuous attention during the match, and among these factors is the cheering of the audience, which is often a burden on the

minds of the players in terms of attention, concentration, and the nervous pressure that it imposes on the players, which results in many

mistakes during the game. And the coach's instructions, as they may also cause the players to be distracted, especially if those instructions place blame on the players or demand a specific performance that they cannot perform during the game, which makes the players distracted and not focused on the performance they are doing, and the match referee's decisions are also the referee's decisions, as It was unfair from the players' point of view, and the players' minds became attached to his decisions

This makes them not well focused on the events of the match, which results in their being distracted in many of the decisions they make or not paying attention to some of the playing situations in general, and our thoughts, feelings and impressions. Sometimes before some matches we have some impressions and feelings towards that match in terms of the opposing team and its capabilities or The importance of the outcome of the match for the team,

or the fact that the players are loaded with certain ideas by the coach in general, are all matters that are either positive and benefit the interest of the team and support its ability to play, or they are negative that cause the team to fail from a mental standpoint, which results in a lack of attention and concentration in performance, which results in... Many technical and tactical mistakes during the game. These examples are examples and are not limited to them, but they draw our attention to the fact that attention has many factors that will affect the players' performance during the matches. In the end, we can say that all of them are things that may cause our train of thought to deviate from its path. During the match, what requires us, while developing the attention performance of the players during exercises and training, is to keep these factors in mind so that we can

Factors affecting sustained attention

There are many and varied factors that help draw attention to the topic and make it capture our attention. These factors can be divided into two basic parts

First : External attention

1. The intensity of the stimulus

The intensity of the stimulus affects attention, such as loud sound, strong smell, and bright light And quick performance through movements, running, and the speed of the ball all take our attention and make us focus on it for a longer period of time than those monotonous and traditional movements and read passes that are useless from our point of view and make us stop paying attention to them.

1. The novelty of the stimulus

New stimuli arouse the individual's attention. When a new guest enters the classroom, he attracts attention Learners because it is exciting and new, also in football when the performance is characterized by play that includes passes that are unique and modern in relation to our experiences, as well as smart and unconventional moves and tactics that are characterized by modernity in terms of all freedom of performance.Things that make our attention and our state of alertness at its peak and with high efficiency. For example, when you find one of the players on the opposing team performing unique and new individual skills, you naturally pay attention to him and be careful of him while you are defending against him, which increases your alertness to avoid him passing you during Attacking with the ball, this is also the case when you find the opposing team performing smart moves and high tactics, this calls for your vigilance and attention to continue their work accurately to avoid mistakes. On the other hand, when you and your teammates during the match perform a new tactical duty in the attack or make a group of passes. Positively, longitudinally, at the opponent's

goal, somewhat quickly, this action also calls for your vigilance and attention.

1.   Change of stimulus

We do not feel the ticking of the clock in the room, but if it stops suddenly, our attention turns to it (Al-Zahir, 2012: 103) This also applies to performance in football. Sometimes we are not attentive to the movements of some of our colleagues on the field because in many playing situations they have become reserved for us and therefore they do not attract our attention, especially if the playing situation does not require abilities.Those players, as for the players whose movements we cannot determine and predict, as they are distinguished by innovation and

diversification in their movements and style of play, prompt us to pay attention to them at all times, and this is what must be done by the players, as it is necessary to change and diversify their style of play, and for it not to be specific or limited, as is said in Among the public (open books do not attract readers), so be a closed book in order to attract them. Do not make your style on the field calculated by your colleagues so that he cannot build the probabilities and results of every pass he makes to you, or that may push him not to pass to you more often.

1. Repetition of the stimulus

Repeating the alarm sound several times is a reason to attract attention, either if the alarm continues to repeat on A single pace has lost its ability to call attention, so the alarm must be varied in issuing it. This is the same case in football, where a performance that is at one pace in terms of speed, whether in passing or movement, does not make us call for our alertness and attention in the required manner. This is in contrast to the varied performance that includes...

A change in the type of passes, where one is longitudinal, the other is transverse, and one is opposite the direction of play, and the various movements that include various tactical aspects between the lines of play make us require greater alertness and attention for longer periods during situations.

Different games, and this is what calls us to the necessity of diversification when building training, to be complex in terms of speeds, required performances, and requirements. Also, when building game plans, the coach must also consider the factor of alertness and attention among the players so that he sets the tactical aspects in a fixed manner so that the players can memorize them, such as) 2 4 4) But it is necessary to diversify the way it is performed and trained in order to impose on the players greater vigilance and constant attention.

1. Location of the stimulus

The more the stimulus is in front of the eye, the more it attracts attention, which is why advertising designers resort to it What is attached to the roads is that advertising should be at the forefront, and these designers know these rules well, whether they are designing advertising signs on the roads or advertisements in newspapers and magazines. Advertising designers know these ideas and make the most efficient use of them in their work, and this is what Kirov, the founder of the rondo exercise, built upon, as in the rondo exercise. The formations are made up of circles or squares in narrow spaces,

where the ball and the attackers are in the eyes of the defenders and vice versa, which makes them need constant vigilance and attention. Also, teams that rely on tiki-taka in their style of playing, you will find them performing this in narrow spaces with great accuracy, on the contrary. When they face a strong team that can distance and separate their lines of play from each other, you find that they are not good at performing passing in the way that they are good at through narrow spaces. This goes back to the narrower the spaces, the more the stimuli represented by the ball, defenders and teammates are in the eye, and this helps in a strong way in summoning... The biggest aspect of constant alertness and attention.

1. Continuity of the stimulus:

As a general rule, the stimulus that lasts longer attracts more attention, because it represents... They insist on the viewer to attract attention.

For example, when a team performs more than one successive pass during an attack, this requires a greater degree of attention from the players,

which makes their concentration of attention higher, as the players begin to focus on their movements well, as well as monitoring the movements of the defending team's defenders, who will increase the rate of their defensive movements in order to extraction

The ball, which is why it is necessary for coaches and players to focus on the type of exercises that depend on the continuity of the stimulus in order to develop their attention-focusing abilities.

1. The size of the stimulus

With regard to visual stimuli, the greater the size of the stimulus, the more it calls for attention and meaning Large-sized stimuli are more attention-grabbing than small-sized stimuli (Rabie, 2011: 100). In football, the stimuli are greater the

closer they are to the players. This is why coaches use narrow spaces in building exercises in order for the stimuli to be close and large, which makes the players more focused and attentive.

1. Contrast

It is anything that is significantly different from what is in its surroundings, for example the appearance of a red dot in the middle It contains black dots (Abdul Wahid, 2006:2).

In football, there are many different stimuli that the coach can introduce in constructing exercises, such as longitudinal and transverse movements, long passes, short passes, fixed goals, moving goals, switching positions between players, and tactical diversification. These are all different forms. The coach can create a weave between some of these types in order to build one exercise.

Second : Internal attention factors

There are various internal factors, temporary or permanent, that prepare the individual to pay attention to special and specific topics and not others

The most important of these factors are the following

1. Motivations, needs and interests

Our interests and motivations determine not only the thing that attracts our attention but the quality of it Stimuli as well. A hungry person is not interested in new clothes, but rather foods and foods. Anything that appeals to our interests, needs, or motivations is valuable to our attention, and we often neglect or ignore many important stimuli because they are outside our circle of attention. This point represents a bottleneck for the coach when constructing exercises, as he must take into account when planning exercises the motivations, needs and interests of each player so that the player can achieve the good and desired benefit from the exercise he performs, as when we look at needs, for example but not limited to, the player's need may be during The game is the need for players to pay attention to his movements on the field or when he takes possession of the ballHe is in need of longitudinal movements from his teammates, as he is good at longitudinal passes, or he does not feel confident in his performance except by performing a large number of passes, or he is not inclined to passes that require greater physical effort. As for interests, for example but not limited to, we find that Some players tend to be more interested in the aesthetics of the performance than its effectiveness, and this is also a problem that must be taken into account while building exercises by building exercises that depend on the effectiveness of the performance more than its aesthetics. As for motivation, we find, for example, but not limited to, that some players tend to play individually through shooting. Or special skills and quirks for the sake of the motivation to prove oneself and stardom in individual performance, and this requires the coach to intervene in building exercises that depend on teamwork and self-denial. In the end, if the motives, needs and interests are not directed in a positive way through the exercises, they stand in the way of the players' attention to many things. Stimuli and incentives that occur during different playing situations.

1. Mental preparation

It is said that mental preparation is the most important internal factor in directing attention. For example, the mother's mental preparation when he lies down. Next to her is her infant. She quickly notices him if he cries, while loud noises do not wake her from her deep slumber. This shows us that it is necessary for coaches to hold group and individual meetings with the players in order to determine the extent and quality of the mental preparation of each player in relation to his teammates on the field, the tactical aspect and other factors. This is in addition to the coach analyzing the performance after the matches to estimate and determine the mental preparation of each player in order to Modifying and evaluating it in a way that develops the player's ability to pay good attention to all stimuli and stimuli and avoid mental preparation based on certain media and public biases, inclinations, or trends, which may cause the player to ignore during the performance in matches many of the important stimuli and stimuli that would affect On the form and result of the match.

1. Level of motivation and internal arousal

There must be a level of motivation or arousal that drives energy The individual's attention is drawn to a specific stimulus. Attention increases as the stimulus increases, and attention decreases if the stimulus decreases.

It is necessary, in order to make the most of the players' attention abilities, whether before training or matches, to renew the players' incentives and create new incentives in line with developing their attention abilities and continuing to perform during matches with high efficiency that suits different playing situations.

1. Previous experience:

If our previous experience with people is that he is a virtuous and benevolent person, then we will pay attention to what he directs to us Whoever gives advice and guidance, or if our previous experience with him is other than that, we will not pay attention to his advice and guidance (Rabie, 2011:

101).This matter is extremely dangerous if the coach does not pay attention to it and address it through training. For example, a player may neglect to pass to one of his teammates who is well positioned inside the opposing team's penalty area simply because his previous experiences confirm to him that if he passes the ball to him, he will not succeed in scoring a goal. That's why he ignores this and passes to another teammate or shoots directly at the goal. The coach can identify these problems through performance analysis. He can also eliminate this problem through players coming together in order to develop each other or through systematic exercises that seek to change the situation. Those bad experiences and replace them with more positive experiences.

Attention components

The attention mechanism consists of searching, filtering, and preparing to respond, which are as follows:

1. Search

The search process is an attempt to determine the location of the stimulus in the visual field, and Posner and his colleagues explained that There are two types of

Searching : The first is extrinsic searching, which occurs involuntarily, such as sudden attention to a flashing light that has appeared in the visual field. The second type is endogenous search, which refers to the process of voluntary, planned search for a stimulus or stimulus with specific characteristics.

1. Liquidation

Ennis and Cameron explain that the filtering process is a process of selecting a stimulus or a specific characteristic And ignoring stimuli or other characteristics that exist in the individual's field of perception.

1. Preparedness to respond:

This process may be called priming, anticipating the appearance of the target, or transforming the target, and it refers to... The individual maintains, changes, or modifies the strategy with which he responded to the previous goal in order to respond to the subsequent goal (Sayyid Ahmed and Badr, 17:1111).

Measurement of sustained attention

Measuring sustained attention is extremely important in football, as through it we can determine our ability to pay good attention over a long period of time.

Secondly, divided attention

The concept of divided attention

The concept of divided attention refers to our brain's ability to pay attention to two different stimuli At the same time, responding to the multiple requirements of the environment surrounding you.

This concept explains that divided attention is a type of simultaneous attention, as it allows us to process different sources of information and successfully perform multiple tasks at the same time. However, let us also know that our ability to pay attention to

multiple stimuli and perform different tasks at the same time has limits that we cannot exceed, as when we divide... Our attention

decreases, and our efficiency in performing these actions decreases, and it is also certain that our performance will be poor, as what is called interference occurs when the brain cannot process all the information present.

However, training can help improve divided attention, allowing us the ability to perform With more than one activity at a time, and when looking at football events, we find that the player always needs the ability to deal with more than one stimulus at a time, and in fact this is what distinguishes

players from each other, as we often find the decisions of some Players lack good vision, which is often caused by the inability of those players to respond to more than one stimulus at a time, which makes their decisions limited only to the stimuli they were able to bring to them. On the contrary, we find some players whose decisions are more visionary, as we can, by watching them, recognize them. Therefore, we often say how the player was able to do this, and this is what shows us the importance of divided attention.

Another concept of divided attention

Divided attention refers to the ability to distribute our attention so that two or more activities can be carried out simultaneously and may use only one sense, such as vision, or two or more senses (Grevas-Down and Carter).

This concept also adds to us that in some situations the individual may rely on one sense to perform more than one activity at the same time, such as the eye, where we can, for example, monitor the field on the left or right side during performance at the same time that we

follow the signals of the coach or colleague who is performing. It refers to us, for example, to clarify the play or in order to pass to it. It also indicates that it may use more than one sense, such as the eye and the ear, as we can monitor the field and performance at the same time as we listen to the instructions of a colleague or coach through the voice.

(Some illustrative examples of divided attention) First example

While we are studying in the classroom, the divided attention is clear and evident through what we practice. The ability to understand what the teacher is saying during the lesson while we are reading the board and taking notes is a clear example where our attention is

divided to deal with two stimuli at the same time, which is understanding what he is saying. The teacher explains at the same time that we are writing down notes on the board, and that the performance of each of us in such a situation varies according to the capabilities we have of divided attention.

Second example

During the match, in many playing situations, we divide our attention so that we can perform correctly. For example, the player in possession of the ball in the attacking midfield often divides his attention between the depth of the field and the left or right side of the field in order to choose the place to run with the ball.

Or the right teammate to pass the ball to, which forces the player to

pay attention to the movements of teammates and opponents on both sides of the game, to whom he divides his attention.

Third example

It is necessary for the waiter (the restaurant worker) to have a good amount of divided attention so that he can remember what the man sitting at table number

(2) wanted and trouble and write down what the man sitting at table number (3) asked for at the same time while he is holding plates of food in his hands. For table number (4), if he does not have the good ability to divide his attention well, he will face many

difficulties in his work, but with training and practice,he will have a good ability, even if this takes a long time, but in the end it is according to his need for that work, which it creates for him. Good motivation that helps him prepare himself to train and do so, and this simple

example shows us that it is necessary to deal with football professionally, which makes us always search for the needs that create in us the motivation and desire to learn with passion and to know that the matter will not stop at the limit of the information we receive from The coach extends to researching and studying this information and knowing its scientific reference and how each of us players can employ it according to his capabilities.

Fourth example

According to the previous example, we also always in football, when we take possession of the ball, we need to follow the movements of our colleagues on the left, right, or deep sides, at the same time that we are required to follow the movements of the opponent's defenders, read those movements, and estimate the distances well, as well as estimate the level of running that we do according to What the playing situation requires in order to resolve the situation, whether by passing, running with the ball, or shooting at the goal, and that any defect in following up on these stimuli causes us to fail in making the appropriate decision, as either losing the ball or performing an ill-considered performance

will result in a random result in the performance, and this imposes a physical and mental tax. Double the team. This is far from wasted time that you were not able to use well due to random performance that is far from attention, awareness, and making correct and quick decisions.

Factors affecting divided attention

There are some other factors, in addition to the general factors we mentioned previously, that affect divided attention. These factors are as follows:

Difficulty of the task

The more difficult and complex the task, the greater the need for focus and cognitive attention. This makes it difficult to divide our attention between multiple tasks

For example, we cannot divide our attention between the goalkeeper's movements, the coach's and players' signals, and the crowd's chants while

executing a penalty kick. If we do that, the result is often unsatisfactory, as the penalty kick requires greater concentration when executing it. Another example is while performing a group of short passes. In front of the opposing team's

penalty area and under strong and strong pressure from the defenders, we cannot divide our attention to see the coach's signals

or listen carefully to the instructions and instructions he tells us.

Similarity of tasks

When tasks are similar, it may become easier to divide attention between the two tasks because the mind does not It requires switching between thinking patterns. However, two similar tasks may compete for the same cognitive resources, which may make dividing attention difficult. For example, when you lead a quick attack with the ball.

While dividing your attention between the running and movement of both the right and left wingers, who run at approximately the same speed and at an equal distance, even though this matter was not exhausting for you, your mind becomes confused as to which of the players has a better chance of passing the ball to him, which makes the task more difficult to concentrate on, which may make it more difficult to concentrate. It results in a passing error due to poor division of attention between two similar tasks.

Importance of the task

We tend to prioritize tasks that we consider to be more important. This sorting of tasks may mean that... Less important tasks do not receive enough attention and lead to mistakes. For example, when you divide your attention between dribbling the defender and then shooting at the goal, and the winger whose movement you are following in order to pass to him, in this case you may prefer to dribble the goalkeeper and then shoot directly at the goal without continuing to look. Or passing to your colleague. This is called prioritizing tasks, as in this case you prioritize direct shooting at the goal instead of passing to your colleague.

In addition, age, experience, and individual differences in cognitive processes can also affect our ability to multitask

Third : Selective attention

The concept of selective attention

It is the process of focusing on a specific object in the environment for a specific period of time. And because Our attention is a limited resource. As we know, selective attention allows us to ignore unimportant details and focus on what is important. It is worth noting at this point that selective attention differs from inattentional blindness, which occurs, as we mentioned previously, when we focus strongly on one thing and fail to notice unexpected things. In our visual field, but it escapes us without us

noticing it.

Another concept of selective attention

In psychology, selective attention is defined as the cognitive process of paying attention to one or fewer sensory stimuli, i.e. external or internal, while ignoring or suppressing all other irrelevant sensory input. The

concept of selective attention in psychology is also called executive attention or controlled attention.

Here we had to clarify the difference between selective attention and divided attention, and we found nothing more than the concept presented to us by Galeotti, which explains the difference between them in a wonderful way.

It indicates that selective attention is the ability to focus on some stimuli at the expense of other stimuli. While he believes that divided attention is the ability to divide attention across different tasks.Through these concepts, it becomes clear to us that selective attention is the ability to select specific stimuli in the environment to process them while ignoring distracting or irrelevant information.At any given moment, we are exposed to a lot of sensory information. For example, while walking down the street, you find the sound of a car horn, an electronic billboard advertising a product, the sound of people sitting in a café while watching a football match, the voice of a flower seller, and some people's quarrels. But in most cases, you do not pay attention to all of it. One of these sensory experiences. Instead, you focus your attention on some important elements in your environment while other things blend into the background or pass by without you completely noticing.

This is the same case in football. For example, during possession of the ball there is a barrage of information. Sensory, such as the coach's instructions to you on the need to pass the ball quickly, your colleague who signals to you with his hand that you must pass it to him, and the team captain who instructs you that it is necessary to pass the ball far from the distance.

The defensive zone, the movements of the defenders, the crowd's chants, and other sensory information, but you cannot focus on all of this. You select what you deem important and the rest goes to the background or you do not see it at all.But here is the important question: How can you ignore some stimuli and focus on only one aspect of your environment ?

We know that our ability to pay attention is limited in terms of effort and duration. Therefore, it is necessary to be selective about what things we pay attention to so that we are not vulnerable to distraction and lack of focus, in addition to mental fatigue resulting from the amount of mental effort expended. This is why selective attention works as a magnifying glass. Or lights, as it highlights the details that we need to focus on and throws irrelevant information to the margins of our awareness. Therefore, in order to focus and maintain our attention, we filter out the things that do not interest us at any moment.

This shows that we focus on some things and ignore other things at the same time. The bottom line is that attention is limited, so it is necessary to focus attention on the most important events. For example, you while playing. It is necessary to pay attention and focus on the tactical aspect well instead of paying attention and focus on

the audience or the referee's decisions that you see as unfair, for example. In the end, you must exploit your ability to pay attention in order to achieve what you want.

Here we had to focus on an important point for us in football

How does selective visual attention work ???????????????????

Since most of the information that players deal with on the field depends on the sense of sight, so scientists were interested in clarifying how selective visual attention works until two main models were reached that describe how visual attention works.

The first model : - highlighting. It suggests that selective visual attention works like a spotlight. It has been suggested that these lights include:

Focus point : The center of focus is known as the focus point, and in this area things appear clear.

Margin : The area surrounding this focal point, known as the margin, is still visible but not clearly visible.

Margin: Finally the area outside the marginal area of the highlight is known as the margin

The second model : - The zoom lens model. It indicates that we are able to increase or decrease the size of our focus just like the zoom lens in a camera, and it explains that the larger the focus area leads to slower processing

because it includes more information,

The second point is how does selective auditory attention work ?????????

One of the most important experiments conducted by scientists at this point is that of scientist Colin Cherry. Cherry investigated how people were able to follow certain conversations while ignoring other conversations, a phenomenon he referred to as the "cocktail party" effect. In this experiment, two audio messages were presented at the same time. One per permission. Sherry then asked the participants to pay attention to a specific message, then what they heard was repeated.

It was discovered that the participants were able to easily pay attention to one message and repeat it, but when they were asked about the content of the other message, they were unable to say anything about it. Sherry also found that when the content of the message was changed Suddenly changing the observation, such as changing from English to Arabic in the middle of the message, was noticed by very few participants. It is interesting to note that when the content of the unattended message was changed from male to female, or the message was changed with a high-pitched tone, the participants noticed the change easily, and the results presented by Sherry have been proven in other experiments.

When we look at football, we find many situations that apply to the results of cocktail party experiments. For example, while grabbing the ball, you are sometimes exposed to two sound stimuli at the same time, such as the sound of a colleague who wants you to pass the ball to him, and another colleague who wants the same thing, but you may You are attracted to someone's call because you are being watched from the first moment you receive the ball, which makes it easier for you to respond to him at the same time that you do not pay attention to the call of your other colleague.

This is on the one hand, and on the other hand, you may pay attention to them both at the same time if the last unattended stimulus is particularly attractive.

Great, such as the intensity and loudness of a teammate's voice, or that he is close to you compared to the monitored stimulus, or that the teammate used a voice that is unfamiliar to you, such as, for example, making the "kiiiiii" Karate shout. This shows us the importance of studying auditory attention, as it enables players to know their abilities in auditory attention and methods. Which increases its intensity, which gives players the ability to attract the

attention of their colleagues in different playing situations in a good way, as many times you need to attract the attention of your colleague in order to pass to him or pass to you, or in order for him or her to move in a certain way.

Factors affecting selective attention

There are many factors that can influence selective attention. Selective attention is concerned with selecting limited stimuli from a large number of stimuli, and external factors are related to the characteristics of the stimuli. It appears that the size, density, and movement of the stimuli are important determinants of attention, as moving, large, shiny, or bright stimuli attract our attention.

We also focus on new and complex stimuli more quickly, as it has been noted that the human image is more susceptible to attention than the image of inanimate objects. Likewise, rhythmic auditory stimuli are attended to more than verbal narration, and

sudden stimuli have a high ability to attract attention to them. The influencing factors are selective attention. In the following: -

Task requirements

The nature of the task at hand affects selective attention. If the task requires concentration On specific details, we are likely to focus our attention on those details and ignore irrelevant information. For example, while reading a book, we selectively pay attention to words and sentences, ignoring background noise.

For example, when taking a penalty kick, we focus on information about the kick, such as the goalkeeper's stance and force. And the accuracy required for implementation, ignoring irrelevant information such as the

cheers of the crowd, the instructions of the coach or a colleague, or any stimulus that the goalkeeper or one of the players of the opposing team tries to perform in order to distract attention.

Individual differences

Each player has a special level and style of selective attention, as some players may have the ability We must focus well and filter out distractions, while others may have difficulty paying attention selectively. This

shows us that many times personal and cognitive traits and attention deficits affect our selective attention, and this matter is clear and evident in many different playing situations. For example, we find some players They have the superior ability to adhere to the tactical instructions that the coach gives them, despite the presence of many distractions that they face during various playing situations. In contrast, we find that some players do not have the ability to adhere to tactical information like the rest of their colleagues, which shows the extent to which they are exposed to many distractions during the game.

Different playing situations.

Emotional state

Emotional factors such as fear, excitement, and other factors can affect attention performance Our selective behavior during the playing situations that we are exposed to during the match, where being guided by our feelings can lead to a

narrow focus on specific aspects of information and stimuli while ignoring others present in the environment. For example, your feeling that you have the ability to score a goal by shooting directly at the opposing team's goal. While you are in possession of the ball in front of the edge of the opposing team's penalty area, this feeling will often make you focusIt depends on the information and stimuli related to shooting, such as the distance, the shooting angle, the force required to shoot the ball with, the goalkeeper's stance, and the shooting angle. At the same time, you ignore the information and stimuli related to the movements of your fellow attackers around you.

Environmental factors

Environmental factors such as noise, visual clutter, and other environmental factors may make us unresponsive While playing, we are able to focus on specific stimuli, as it requires a lot of effort to filter out distractions and selectively pay attention to relevant information and stimuli. For example,often when young players are exposed to playing in

large matches with large crowds, chants, and loud noise, we find their performance is lower and returns. This is because their

attention was distracted as a result of them not being accustomed to playing in the presence of a large crowd and loud voices and chants.

Attention control

Also, the player's ability to control the focus of attention plays an important role in selective attention We find that some players have a superior ability to direct their attention in the desired manner towards relevant stimuli. At the same time, we find that some players face difficulty in maintaining the focus of their attention towards relevant information, and this matter is clear and evident in many different playing situations that require... Players should direct their attention towards specific information and stimuli. At the same time, players should not be exposed to or be led by irrelevant information and stimuli. Among these situations, for example, is when there is a prior agreement between the players on how to execute direct free kicks in front of the opposing team's penalty area, where we find that some players are committed to the agreed- upon performance,while others are led by the incentives present during this situation, as The player may be led by the goalkeeper's stance, as the player deems it appropriate for him to shoot directly at the goal, or he may see his human wall stance as wrong, or he has a specific motive that he wants to do, such as the desire to score a goal in order to top the team's goalscoring list,

or to rank the tournament's top scorers in each tournament. In these situations, the player may succeed or fail, but in the end he failed by not directing attention to the relevant information and stimuli in such a situation, which was agreed upon and rehearsed a lot, and was distracted by other stimuli.

Cognitive load

Cognitive load refers to the amount of cognitive information that must be processed during a task It is possible that information with a high cognitive load may lead to a failure or a reduction in selective attention resources, resulting in the inability to direct selective attention in the required manner according to what the gaming situation requires, while tasks with a low cognitive load allow for better cognitive attention, for example when You are in possession of the ball amid a strong defensive presence by the players of the opposing team, and you want to pass according to an agreed-upon tactical aspect.

This aspect requires you to direct your attention towards the right and left wings. This situation requires a high cognitive load in terms of the spacing of the relevant stimuli, at the same time that the irrelevant stimuli constitute a great burden on you. This may lead to your inability to pay attention with the required selectivity that you must do.

According to the playing situation, and this shows us the necessity of paying attention, when developing the tactical aspects, to the relationship between the cognitive load required for the tactical aspects and the resources that the attention capabilities of the players allow and provide that make them able not to be distracted. This is on the one hand, but the other aspect, which must also be taken into consideration, is that the coaches realize the

relationship.

Between the stimuli within the subject's tactical aspect and the irrelevant external stimuli in terms of similarity, closeness, distances, speeds, and playing situations so that they can reduce the irrelevant stimuli, strengthen and process them, and develop alternative plans to enhance the relevant stimuli within the tactical aspect.

Fourth, alternating attention

The concept of alternating attention

The concept of alternating attention refers to the ability to shift the focus of attention and switch between... Two or more activities with different cognitive requirements. As we often do one activity and switch to another activity, this demonstrates that it is necessary to have mental flexibility to be able to switch between different tasks efficiently without the cognitive burden of one task affecting the performance of other tasks, or switching tasks in itself leading to a change in focus.

Example for clarification: - For example, administrative and office employees can perform work, then stop working to answer the phone and make a call, then resume work again, and such matters require more alternating attention.

Another example to clarify: - People who work in the field of simultaneous translation also need more alternating attention, as they switch between more than one language, such as English and Arabic .

(Illustrative examples through football) First example

For example, while playing, you run with the ball, then you do a visual scan and determine which player you should pass to, then you pass, and then you run without the ball and do a visual scan in order to choose the appropriate place to run through so that you can open a good gap for him to pass. To your colleague, then you receive, then you shoot at the goal, and so on. In these situations, we find a lot of cognitive resources that we are exposed to, as the movements of the defenders and colleagues, the spaces available during the performance, the speed of the ball, the coach's instructions outside the lines, signals from colleagues, the agreed upon tactical aspects, and the speed of performance all require more attention from us. What imposes on us the need to alternate our attention to it so that we can perform well.

Second example

When executing direct free kicks or penalty kicks, as well as goal kicks, you do a visual scan and analyze the situation first, then you implement it. This also represents a switch between tasks, as during the visual scan you read and understand the situation and then proceed to apply and implement the appropriate decision in order to achieve the goal. What we want to say is that even the most difficult play situations require this type of attention, as you switch between tasks during play situations.

Third example

Goalkeeping also requires more alternating attention in all playing situations, whether static, such as direct or indirect free kicks, where the goalkeeper must switch attention between the location of the ball and the positions of the attacking and defending players, attacking, or moving, whether it is an organized attack or a lightning attack, where the goalkeeper must The goal is to read the attackers' movements as well as direct his teammates, which requires switching attention to the right, left, and depth in terms of the movements of teammates and opponents at all times.

Factors affecting alternating attention

There are some factors that will affect our alternating attention performance while switching between different tasks, and these factors can be summarized as follows

Working memory capacity

It is a temporary storage system that processes sensory memory, which is considered a very short storage process, as sensory memory can retain visual information for half a second and auditory information for a few seconds.

Working memory

also represents the bridge between the information that is received from sensory memory and the permanent storage of information in Long-term memory is called working memory because it represents the system in which memory work occurs. If you want to retrieve information from long-term memory, you transfer it to your working memory, where you can think about that information, as it represents the conscious repetition of information. Short- term memory often requires conscious effort and use. Suitable for alternating attention, as our working memory is limited in capacity, and therefore it is not good when our alternating attention is directed towards more than one new and stressful task, because that requires more mental effort.Therefore, it is necessary to take into account the players' working memory capacity when planning complex skill exercises or performances. Plans to develop alternating attention and working memory together.

Processing speed

Processing speed is a cognitive ability, which is the time it takes a person to perform a mental task, as it is related to the speed with which a person can understand the information he receives or interact with, whether it is visual or auditory. In other words, it is the time between receiving a stimulus and responding to it, and this is why when switching attention. Between more than one stimulus depends on the speed of our information processing. If the speed of information processing is not good, this will affect our ability to switch between different tasks.

Difficulty of tasks: - As we explained previously, we cannot pay attention and focus on more than one task that requires great mental effort, as this leads us to unintentional blindness and thus increases the difficulty of switching our attention on different tasks.

Planning football training according to attention

First / Rondo exercise

After we finished clarifying the concept of attention and its types, how each type works and the factors affecting it, and how attention affects the players' abilities during play in terms of technical, physical and tactical abilities through a detailed explanation mixed with examples through which we were able to clarify the relationship between fast and slow thinking with regard to attention and control. In it, it was necessary to direct the benefit of this information and knowledge towards how to build and plan football training exercises in a way that allows us to develop and control attention and its types. Hence, we must first study and discuss the current exercises that are being developed to develop the technical, physical and tactical capabilities of players and whether they are compatible with the idea of developing attention. Control it or not???? Then we can do what is necessary to develop our attention capabilities through exercises.There is no one in the field of football who does not know the rondo exercise, and everyone knows that it is one of the most important modern exercises in football, but let me ask a question.

Does the rondo exercise allow players to develop and control attention or not ???

From that point, in order to clarify this, we must explain the Rondo exercise in order to answer that question.

First, the concept of the rondo exercise

It is an exercise in which a group of players possess the ball while being outnumbered Another group. The primary goal of the group with the largest number is to keep the ball, while the goal of

the smaller group is to recover the ball.

The most important thing the coaches said about rondo training

Laureano Ruiz, the inventor of the rondo exercise, says: If a child can perform well in this exercise, he has enough to become a professional player.

When Johan Cruyff started using the rondo, he said, "Do not lose the ball and let it run, for it does not get tired."

Kirov says that everything that happens in the match, except for shooting, you can do in the rondo exercise, whether from the competitive side or the technical side, where you can do the following

What do you do when you have the ball? What do you do when you don't have the ball?

How can you recover and extract the ball from the opponent?

How can you receive and pass with one touch?

Guardiola also says in Simon Cooper's book (Men of Football): Without the ball, we are a terrible team, so we need the ball. He refers to Barcelona's less physical aspect and superior technical ability against opponents. He also says what I learned here is that everything begins with the ball and ends with the ball. We try to We keep this ball, try to play with this ball, try to do everything with the ball. This is what we learned when we were young.

Methods and models for performing the rondo exercise

The Rondo exercise is performed according to geometric shapes such as a circle, square, or rectangle Or a triangle or a trapezoid, and these geometric shapes are of different sizes depending on the goal of the exercise and the players' technical and physical level and their ages. The performance takes place between the two largest groups, which are in possession of the ball and exchange passes between them, whether from one touch or from two touches, according to the requirements of the exercise, and the player who He who loses the ball becomes a defender, or the player who recovers the ball takes his place.

What makes the rondo exercise different from other possession exercises is that the players occupy pre-defined spaces instead of stagnating in every place.

Examples of the rondo exercise include (2*6) (3*6) (2*5) (4*2) (3*1)

When we take an analytical look at the rondo exercise, we find the following

First, the rondo exercise is based on centralization

As the rondo exercise is planned according to geometric shapes such as Square, circle, rectangle, triangle...etc.

Although this is very good as it prevents players from moving to spaces that are not closely related to technical performance during training, which saves players from exerting great physical effort, which reduces the technical returns of passing, this makes it The exercise is a closed circuit, where the defenders are in the center of the geometric shape under the eyes of the attackers, and vice versa, the attackers are in a fixed field of vision for the defenders, which reduces the stimulation of their attention.

And the extent of their readiness of alertness, as all stimuli are located in the field of vision, which makes the exercise ignore the development of types of attention such as divided, selective, or alternating attention, which we previously explained the use of each entity during play through the examples we mentioned of each type of attention. This is what makes it important.

Players are limited to the accuracy and speed of receiving and passing. This work is similar, for example, to training for shooting players who train on fixed targets, where their focus is on shooting techniques (skill). On the contrary, when training is on moving targets, it requires attention and vigilance to the stimuli (moving targets).

For the sake of speed and accuracy in responding to it and making the correct shot at it, which makes the shooter care more about the cognitive processes represented by attention and concentration. This is also the case in football, but it increases the difficulty since in a football match you will not find a geometric shape agreed upon in advance or you are passing from a standstill. Most of the time, the position of the defenders is specified in the middle, where things are different, there are more and unexpected stimuli, and fast and different movements that require all types of attention in order to behave well and make appropriate decisions with each of the playing situations that change with every second that passes during the game.

Secondly, the rondo exercise does not develop the technical aspect of the players

Looking at the performance in the rondo exercise, we find that we are... In order to master the rondo, we only need mastery of the receiving and passing mechanism, as we do not need a strong mobilization of attention or concentration as in real playing situations in matches. This shows us that the rondo helps us develop the same skill in its first form under difficult circumstances represented by pressure from defenders.

But in isolation from what actually happens in the matches, he does not care about developing our technical side during training in terms of positions, movements, visual scanning, and monitoring.

This is what makes the rondo exercise limited to the skill side, away from the technical side, and this is what makes it clear to us that the rondo exercise is It requires great technical aspects in order to master it and achieve the goals of the exercise, whether those aspects relate to the player or the group, and the matter is not related to mastering the skill of receiving and passing or the method of defending against attackers, but rather this is due to the necessity of paying attention to the technical aspect represented by mental aspects such as attention and concentration in terms of the degree The mental effort required by each of the different playing situations. For example, in playing situations that require good skill in receiving and passing, they also require technique in movements and positions, a good ability to pay attention to stimuli that arise during the playing situation, good handling, and making good and quick decisions, and this in turn requires effort. Great mental effort. In the end, we can say that the rondo needs modification that allows for the development of slow thinking abilities, represented by attention, control, and mental effort, so that we can finally find players who can perform the skills automatically under the banner of the mind, represented by the technical aspect of the player in terms of attention, focus, and intelligence. Play .

How to develop the Rondo exercise according to the capabilities, types, and control of attention

After we have clarified the most important points that affect Given the extent of the benefit of the rondo exercise from a mental and technical standpoint, on the one hand, and the importance of the rondo exercise in terms of developing the skill aspects well, we had to add some changes and modifications to the way the rondo exercise is planned, in a way that allows us to develop the players' slow and fast thinking abilities. Through the Rondo exercise, here are the most important changes and modifications

First : Providing incentives and stimuli during training, just as they stimulate actual performance in matches. For example, it is unreasonable in matches for the defenders to be positioned in the middle of the attackers in possession of the ball all the time. The exact opposite

happens in matches, where the defenders chase the attackers from all sides, from the front and from the back. From the right and the left,

this is what makes the centralization of the rondo in its traditional sense unjustified.

This exercise must depend on conditional decentralization that allows the players a good amount of freedom of movement while maintaining the skill objectives of the exercise because it is unrealistic for the movements of the players in possession of the ball to be restricted in the presence of... Defense is spread everywhere on the field. Therefore, it is necessary to have a great deal of freedom of movement during training, whether for attackers or defenders, in order to activate the role of realism in training, which helps develop the players' mental, technical, physical, and tactical performance in a way that is compatible with the course of play in the actual matches.

For this reason, we have set some points that help us activate the conditional freedom of the players in the rondo exercise, as follows

- The performance is performed in square, triangle, and circle geshapes, as is the case in the traditional rondo exercise, but not from stability, but rather from movement along the length and breadth of the court, while maintaining the geometric shape

- during performance, as well as maintaining the area tometric

hat the coach sets in order to preserve the identity of the exercise, which has goals. This is good, provided that the coach pays attention to the necessity of diversifying the playing space within one exercise, even if it is roughly, it is much better than consistency.

For example, it is possible to place a specific space for each line of the field. In building the game from the back line, the space will be somewhat larger. The space in the middle is noticeably small in the attacking line, and it brings several benefits to the players, including that it helps the attacking players to get used to building geometric shapes during play, and this provides the players with complete flow and ease in performance, especially the tactical one, which encourages building exercises in this way. It makes the players communicate and understand more with each other, and this will help them to converge mentally and tactically during the performance. This also helps them save the mental effort that the players expend in order to build an organized attack away from randomness in the performance, and this also makes them not make a great physical effort in order to Organizing and managing the attack, which requires a higher effort in the case of random decisions made by the players, as one decision is made byIf one player is wrong, it costs the players more mental and physical effort. It also helps the defensive players and develops their performance in how to dismantle those geometric shapes during play. It also develops their ability to defend against an organized attack and develop the skill of visual scanning, and it also increases the incentives and stimuli. In the exercise where the movements are unexpected.

- Attacking players are tasked with building more than one geometric shape during a single exercise, which allows players when switching from one geometric shape to another, such as switching from a square to a circle, to pay a great deal of attention and direct it during the switching process.

- This is also a realistic matter commensurate with the playing conditions that force players Performing shifts in movement and positioning during performance helps players achieve harmony and fluidity in performing those movements and positions required by

playing conditions.

- The exercise determines the time and number of tasks assigned to the players, so that the relationship between the two elements allows the introduction of more stimuli and incentives that match the realism of the game.

-Some playing situations must be provided that require appropriate mental effort to play

- The exercise must have a clear and decisive end for the group and not for the individual

- To build on the basis of gradation from difficult to easy with regard to the two functions of the mind, slow and fast thinking .

Models for developing the Rondo exercise according to attention capabilities, types, and control

First exercise

Exercise name : Rondo 2*4

The goal of the exercise : developing constant attention to players - developing passing and receiving

Equipment and tools : football field - soccer ball - handball - small goal - whistle

Organization and preparation : The coach defines a square 20 x 20 m. On its sides are four attacking players who hold one soccer ball, and in the middle of the square are two defensive players wearing numbered shirts (2:1), one of

whom takes possession of a handball.

The coach places a small goal at one end of the field.

Instructions : At the start signal, the attacking players exchange passes and move from the square towards the goal, while maintaining the distance between

them and not increasing the distance between them, and being alert and paying attention to the ball possessed by the number one defender, as the defenders

work to distract the attackers by exchanging handball passes among themselves, as well as Exchanging passes with the attackers, and here it is necessary for the attacker in possession of the ball to mention the number of the player to whom he passes the handball.

This requires the attacking players to be more alert in order to pass and follow the path of the handball as well

The second exercise

Exercise name : 6*3 + Joker

The goal of the exercise : Developing players' continuous focus of attention - developing passing and receiving.

Equipment and tools : football field - football - colored cones - small goals

Organization and preparation : The attacking players stand in a circle, possessing a soccer ball, the defending players in the middle of the circle, and the joker player outside the circle. The coach places colored flags in a spread, red, blue, and yellow, then places a small goal on each side of the touchline,

and also places at the end of the ball. The field at the goal line is a small goal

Instructions : At the start signal, the attacking players exchange passing and receiving among themselves and move towards the goals as follows. If the

joker player centers next to a blue funnel, the attacking players move in a circle towards the goal located on the right of the field, and if he focuses towards the green funnel, the attackers move in a rectangle towards the goal located in To the left of the field, and if he rests next to a red funnel, the attackers move in two small triangles towards the goal at the end of the field. If the joker rests on one foot, this means it is necessary for the attacking player to pass the ball tohim very quickly, as the joker works to distract the players, which makes them In a state of alertness and high concentration of attention..

Third exercise

Exercise name : Control group and experimental group

The goal of the exercise : developing the players' divided attention - developing passing and receiving skills

Tools and equipment : football field - ball whistle

Organization and preparation : The players are divided into two adjacent groups, ten meters apart

The first group, which is the control group in red, consists of 2 * 9, meaning two defenders against five attackers

The second group is in blue 3 * 9. A goal is placed for each group at the end of the field

Instructions : At a signal, each group performs the rondo, passing and receiving from the movement to reach its goal. The experimental group must pay attention to the geometric shape in which the control group performs, as it is

necessary for the experimental group to work in the same geometric shape in which the control group performs. For example, if the control group changes the geometric shape from a square to a circle, the experimental group must change it to the same geometric shape, and so on, as the control group works to diversify the geometric shapes through which it leads in order to reach the goal. This forces the experimental group to further divide Attention is given as the number of defenders is greater and it also needs to be followed up by the control group.

Fourth exercise Exercise name : Choosing numbers

Exercise type : Rondo

The goal of the exercise: developing selective attention - developing passing and receiving with the soles of the feet

Organization and preparation : The players are divided into (3) attackers wearing shirts numbered (1:3) in the form of a circle.

And (3) defenders in the middle of the circle. The attacking players possess two numbered balls (1:2). The coach places a small goal at the end of the field.

Instructions : At the start signal, the attacking players exchange passes as follows: The player to whom the ball is passed number (1) receives it and passes it back to any attacking player wearing an individual shirt until the

number of passes reaches three, then to the player who receives the ball number one. After the three passes, he passes it to a player wearing a doubles shirt.

The player to whom the ball is passed number (2) must receive it and pass it back to any player wearing this doubles shirt until the number of passes

reaches four passes. Then the player who receives ball number two after the four passes must pass it to a player wearing an odd shirt.

Fifth exercise Exercise name : Geometric scrolling

Type of exercise : Rondo alternating attention

The goal of the exercise : developing alternating attention - developing passing and receiving with the soles of the feet

Tools and equipment : soccer field - soccer ball - whistle

Organization and preparation : The players are divided into (6) attackers and

(2) defenders in a circle. The attacking players take possession of one soccer ball.

The coach places a small goal at one end of the field

Instructions : The attacking players exchange passes in order to reach the goal as follows When the attackers reach five passes, they must change the

organization from a circle to a square with a half-side, then they count the passes again until they reach seven passes, where they must change the geometric shape from a square with a half-side to two triangles, then the attackers repeat the passes until they reach nine. Passes where they have to

change the shape to a rectangle, and so on until they reach the goal, and this requires players to pay more attention, alternating between tasks and stimuli.

secondly / How to develop exercises through basic skills training methodsAccording to the attention capabilities of the players

Methods of training basic skills in football

- Feeling exercises "getting used to the ball".

- Mandatory technical exercises.

- Exercises with more than one ball.

- Teaching basic skills while linking this to the development of physical qualities.

- Compound exercises.

- Basic skills training using small games.

- Training in basic skills using devices and tools.

The basic principles that must be present in exercises and training within each method of training basic skills : -

1- Taking into account the attention and control capabilities of players 2- Strive to develop all types of attention.

1. It should be built on a sound scientific and practical basis.
2. Diversity of teaching methods, such as problem solving, trial and error, and exploration, all of which are ways that make the learner active Conscious

thinking, which helps players use their thinking abilities well and effectively to suit different playing situations.

1. It should be appropriate to the players' abilities and take into account their individual differences, especially with regard to slow and fast thinking abilities I have the players.

1. It must suit the nature of play and competition so that it is not far-fetched and unrealistic, but rather it must be more realistic It occurs in the course of play and variables that require conscious attention and mental effort.
2. It provides security and safety.
3. There is joy and happiness in it.
4. It suits the players' inclinations, desires and interests, which helps develop attention and response to all stimuli and incentives. Various things that come up during play.

The basic skills in football are divided into two basic types as follows

[1] Basic football skills:-

Hitting the ball with the foot

- Running with the ball.

- Dodge.

- Control the ball.

- Heading the ball.

- Attacking.

- Throw-in.

- Goalkeeping.

[2] Basic physical skills : -

- Running and changing direction.

- Jumping.

- Deception and camouflage with the body.

- Defensive player and goalkeeper stance.

When talking about ball strikes, we find that they are divided into

A - Scrolling. B - Correction. C - Distraction.

Here we will take the skill of passing with the sole of the foot as a skill model during the process of developing attention within the methods of training in basic football skills.

Examples of exercises to develop sustained attention through basic skills training methods

First: ball sense exercises

Ball feeling exercises teach players the properties of the ball in terms of weight, size, and air pressure of the ball, as well as its speed, whether on the ground or in the air. Lack of mastery of feeling and handling of the ball is considered a major obstacle in learning and applying many basic skills such as receiving the ball or hitting the ball (passing and shooting). - Distraction or dribbling with the ball Therefore, it is considered one of the most important methods of training in basic skills, especially in the budding and junior stages, and for this reason it was necessary to begin the process of developing continuous attention through training from the first method of continuous training, not only because it is important, but also because continuous attention is no less important in practicing. Football, where the player needs to develop in order to be able to deal with many playing situations that depend mainly on the capabilities of continuous attention, as players are always in need of continuous attention, whether it is at the level of alertness, which represents the basic stage of continuous attention, which is represented by the players' ability To discover the new incentives that they are exposed to with each of the different playing situations, as football is characterized by speed and change in terms of

physical, skill and tactical performance with each of the different playing situations,

or in the level of concentration of attention, or concentration that allows us to focus our attention on this. Motivation during play. For example, during play, you are required to follow the position of the ball and the movements of teammates and competitors. You respond to every stimulus issued by them and realize whether it needs to be focused on or to continue paying attention to the playing situation in general, and so on during different playing situations, and in order to develop attention during training methods. Regarding basic skills, it is necessary for there to be consistency between skill performance and mental performance, represented by attention, meaning that the development of attention should progress from easy to difficult, and from simple to complex, such as skill performance during training methods for basic skills. Therefore, in the first training method, represented by sensation, You find the process of developing attention very simple, then the difficulty increases in each method of training basic skills.

A - Scrolling. B - Correction. C - Distraction.

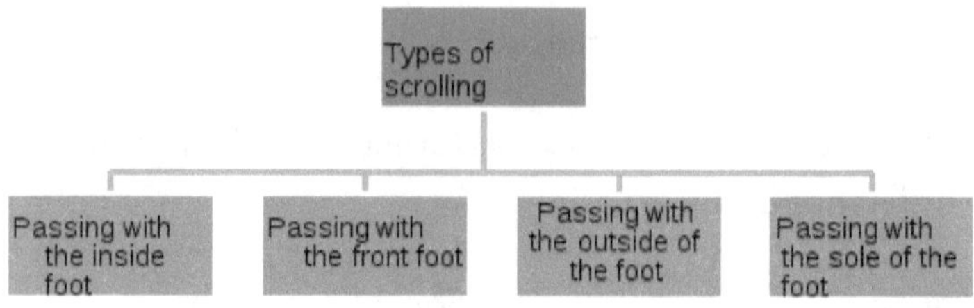

Exercise (1)

Exercise name : What did you see?

The goal of the exercise : developing constant attention to players - developing sense of the ball

Equipment and tools : 20*20 field - football - phone or screen with video clips recorded, the duration of the video ranging between 60:30 seconds - whistle.

Organization and preparation : The players stand in a row. The distance between each player and the other is (5) meters, and in front of them at a distance of (15) meters. A screen or mobile phone is placed at a height appropriate to head level.

Each player has possession of a ball.

Instructions : At the start signal, each player dribbles the ball with his front foot while trying to follow the video that the coach is playing on the video screen, where the video displays different shapes for a minute. The performance is repeated while changing the

content of the display, and so on, as it is necessary for each player to mention what he sees in the video. While he is dribbling the ball, knowing that the video contains images of different things and different colors, the difficulty of the exercise can be increased by increasing the speed of changing images on the screen or adding complex and difficult images .

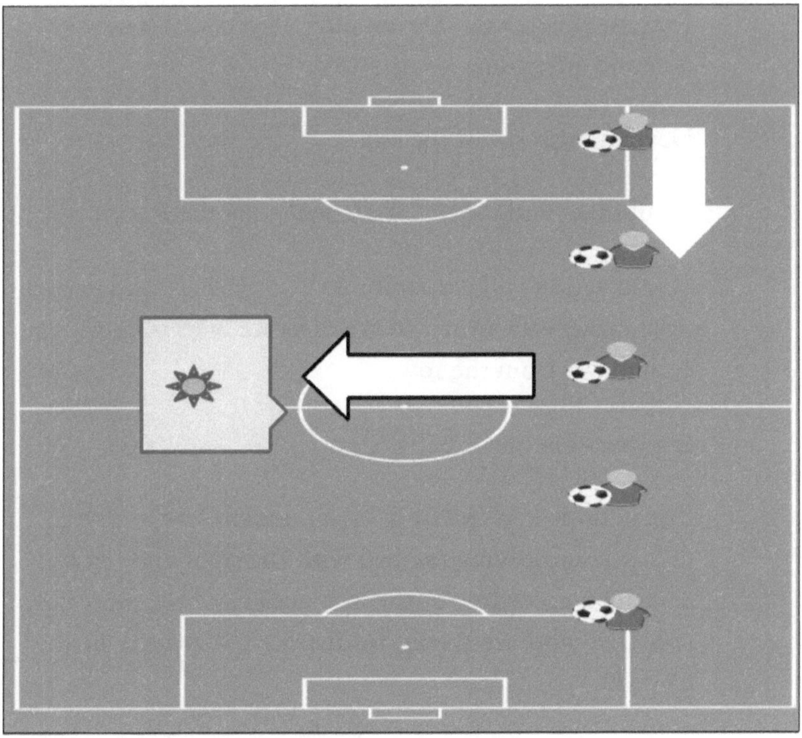

5
M

VIDEO
M 15

Exercise (2) Exercise name : Ball dribbling instructions

Type of exercise : ball sensation exercise

Exercise objectives : Developing players' constant alertness and attention -

Developing sense of the ball

Equipment and tools : 20*20 field – footballs – whistle

Organization and preparation : The players stand in two rows facing each other, with a distance of (5 m) between each player from the row

In possession of the ball (A)

Instructions : At the start signal, the players in row (A) take turns dribbling the ball with the right and left foot and thigh according to the instructions of the players in row (B), who are trying to distract the players in row (A). The

player who makes a mistake in implementing the instructions of the player facing him in the other row switches with him and becomes the player. The person facing him is responsible for dribbling the ball, and the player at fault performs the instructions .

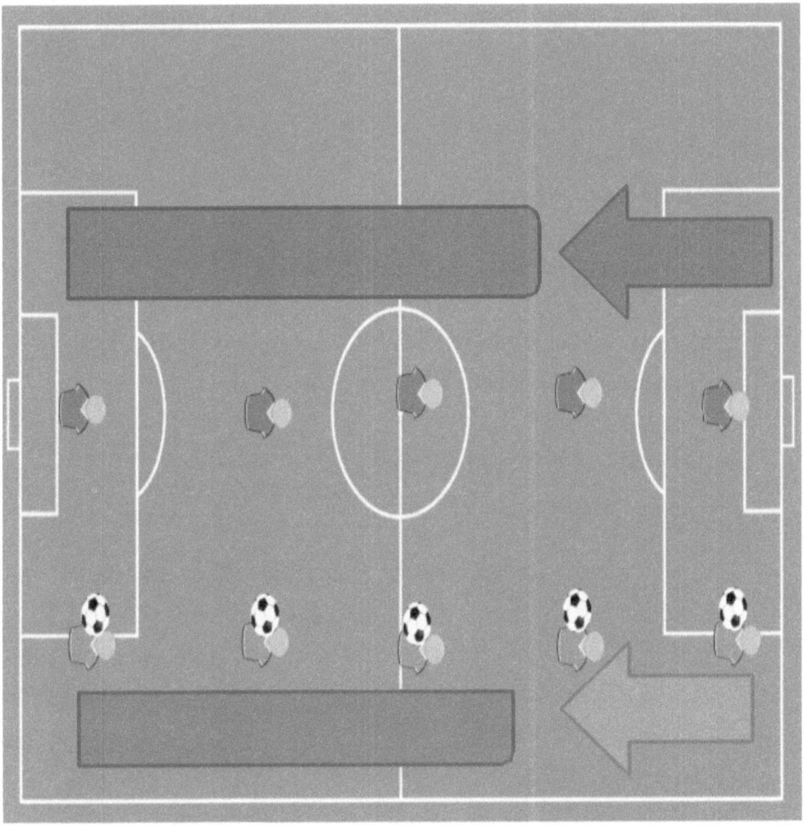

ROW (B)

ROW (

A)

Exercise (3)

Exercise name : Joker cones

Type of exercise : ball sensation exercise

Exercise objectives : Developing players' constant alertness and attention - Developing sense of the ball

Equipment and tools : 20*20 field – footballs – colored cones – whistle

Organization and preparation : The players stand freely spread across the field, and each player is in possession of a ball The joker player stands in the middle of a 5*5 square marked with colored cones

Instructions : At the start signal, the players dribble the ball with the right

and left foot, the thigh, and the head according to the movements of the joker player towards the cones of the square. For example, if it rests next to the small red cone, the players dribble the ball with the thigh - if it rests on the small red cone, they dribble with the right foot - and the blue-green cone with the foot. The left side - and the yellow funnel on the head

The joker is trying to distract the players

Players pay attention to goker during the

Square 5 * 5 m

As aresult the joker running towards the small red funnel , the players dribble the ball with their thighs

EXERCISE (4) EXERCISE name : Reverse the coach's signal.

Exercise type : Ball sensation exercise

Objective of the exercise : Developing vigilance and constant attention to players - developing sense of the ball.

Equipment and tools : soccer field - soccer balls.

Organization and preparation : The players stand freely spread across the field, each player in possession of a football

Instructions : At the start signal, each player alternates passing the ball between the right and left foot, paying attention to the coach's signals, in order

to run during the performance, contrary to the coach's signal. For example, if he points with his hand to the back, the players run to the left during the performance, and so on.

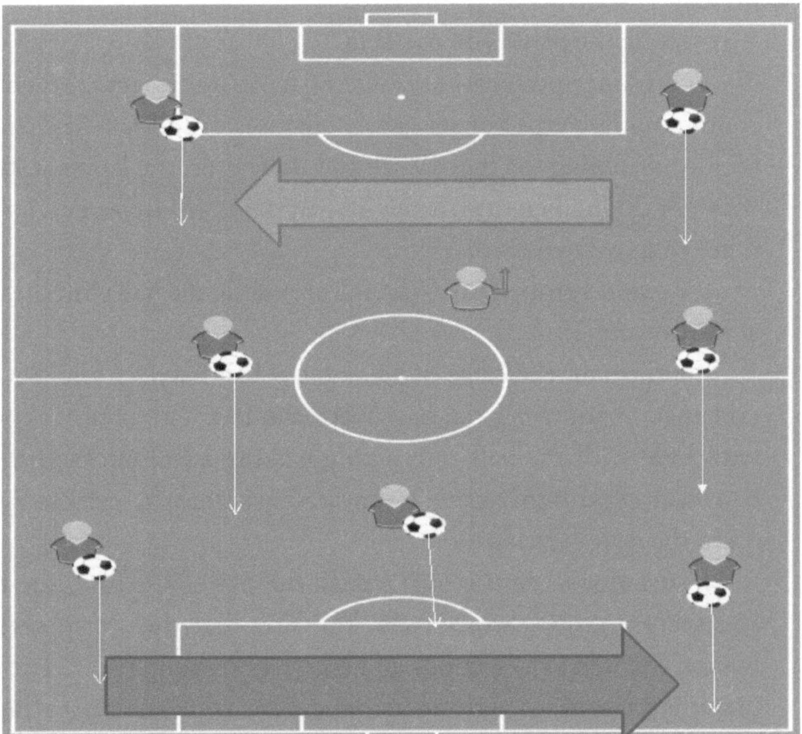

The coach is try to deceive the players

The players perform against the direction of coach' s hand

EXERCISE (5) EXERCISE name : Sensation groups

Exercise type : Ball sensation exercise

Objective of the exercise : Developing players' concentration of attention - developing a sense of the ball.

Equipment and tools : stadium20*20 – Footballs – Whistle.

Organization and preparation : The players stand freely spread out on the field, each player has possession of the ball, the coach is present

Among the players on the field

The trainer performs two sets of sensation exercises, each set containing five types of sensation exercises as followsThe first assembly, dribbling the ball (With the right foot, the left foot, then the right thigh, then the left thigh, then the head) Repeat each type twice to move to the other type.

the second group (An exchange of pulling the ball with the feet at the bottom of

the shoe, an exchange of passing the ball between the feet, an exchange of touching the ball With the feet, alternate making a semicircle with the ball, alternating making a full circle with the ball)Each type in this group is repeated five times in order to move on to the next exercise.

Instructions : At the start signal, the players perform the first and second group, respectively, knowing that the group performance The first (15) seconds and the second group (30). Here the player is attentive to performance and time, which increases the focus of his attention in order to succeed in the task.

The coach monitors the extent of players' attention while performing exercise groups

Exercise (6)

EXERCISE NAME : ATTENTION signal and sound. Exercise type:Ball sensation exercise

Objective of the exercise : Developing players' concentration of attention - developing a sense of the ball.

Equipment and tools : Football field - colored cones - footballs - whistle

Organization and preparation : The players stand in a line behind the starting line, and each player is in possession of a soccer ball.

The coach places colored cones at equal distances along the length of the field, and the distance between one cone and the other is 20

meters, numbered in ascending order from (1:6).

- Red: The player in the space between him and the next funnel alternates passing the ball between the running feet.

- Yellow: He alternates dribbling the ball with his feet, whether walking or running.

 - Blue: Dribble the ball with the right foot three times and with the left foot three times in a row. The coach stands at the end of the field with three red, yellow, and blue cones in front of him. If the coach leans toward the blue cone and says, "Blue (6), this means that the players must perform the exercises specific to the blue color, from running until they reach the blue cone number (6), and so on.

Instructions: The coach focuses on the players' need to perform the exercises for each color of funnel well, while paying attention to the coach's signals .

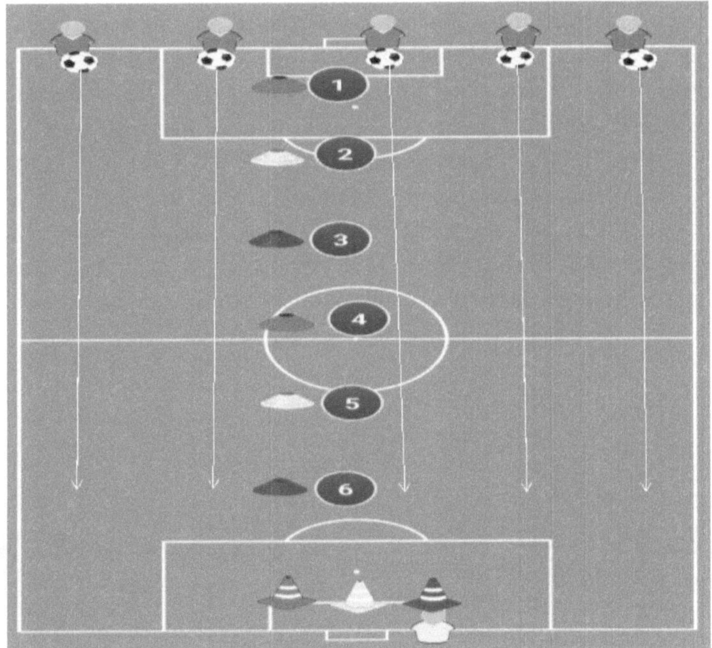

Exercise (7)

EXERCISE NAME : ARRANGING the balls

Type of exercise : Exercise with more than one ball

The goal of the exercise : developing alertness and concentration of attention for players - developing passing with the sole of the foot

Equipment and tools : playground25*25 – numbered footballs – numbered cones – whistle Organization and preparation : The players stand in two locomotives facing each other (: AB) The distance between them is 15 metres

Five numbered cones are placed in front of each locomotive in a random order, let them be (5, 3, 1, 4, 2), with the distance between each cone being (50) cm. They are placed in front of the locomotive.A) Five footballs, numbered 1:5, also in random order.

Instructions : At the start signal, the first player from the locomotive (A) The red one passes

the balls in a random order, each ball toward the cone that matches it in number according to the movement of the first player from the cone. (B) The blue one tries to distract the player passing him by leaning toward the numbered cone. If he leans toward the cone number one on the lane, the ball number one is passed. Where the first player from the locomotive (B) receives the five balls in this manner, then they exchange roles, where the recipient becomes a passer and vice versa. Then each player returns to the last of his locomotive, so that the second player from each locomotive begins, and so on.

The receiving player always tries to distract the passer, as we can see in the picture. When the receiving player leaned towards funnel number one, the passer passed the ball towards funnel number one, and so on.

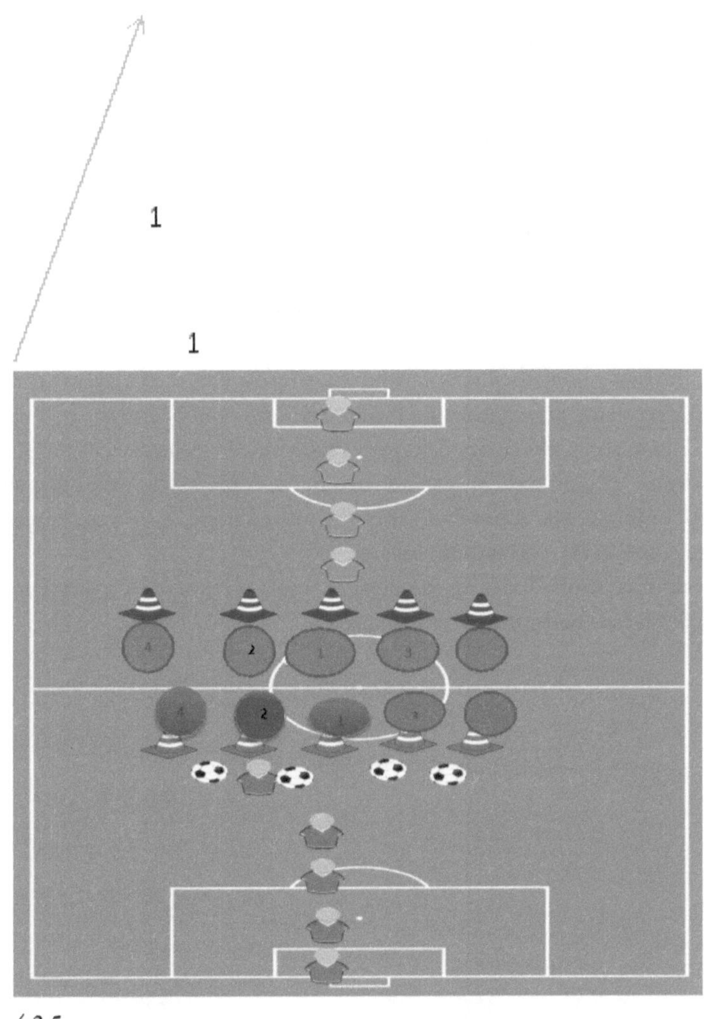

Exercise (8)

Exercise name : A square within a square Type of training : Compulsory technical

The goal of the exercise : developing vigilance and constant attention to players - developing passing with the sole of the foot

Equipment and tools: football field - cones - footballs

Organization and preparation : The trainer draws a large square30*30, resting on its sides are four players wearing red shirts numbered from (1:4). It is called the square (A), and

inside it is a small square with an area of 15*15 m, with the same formation and numbers of the players, called the square (B). Its players wear blue shirts. Each square takes possession of His players are on one football

Instructions : At the start signal, the players of each square exchange passes with the sole

of the foot among themselves. When passing the ball, each player tries to distract the receiving player. After performing the pass and before the ball reaches the receiving player, the passer determines the number of the player to whom the receiving player must pass. He can also determine A player from the other square says, for example, player number three, the other square, and so the players exchange passes in this way in both squares.

Technical points: Focus on the alertness and attention of the players and the correct technical performance of the pass

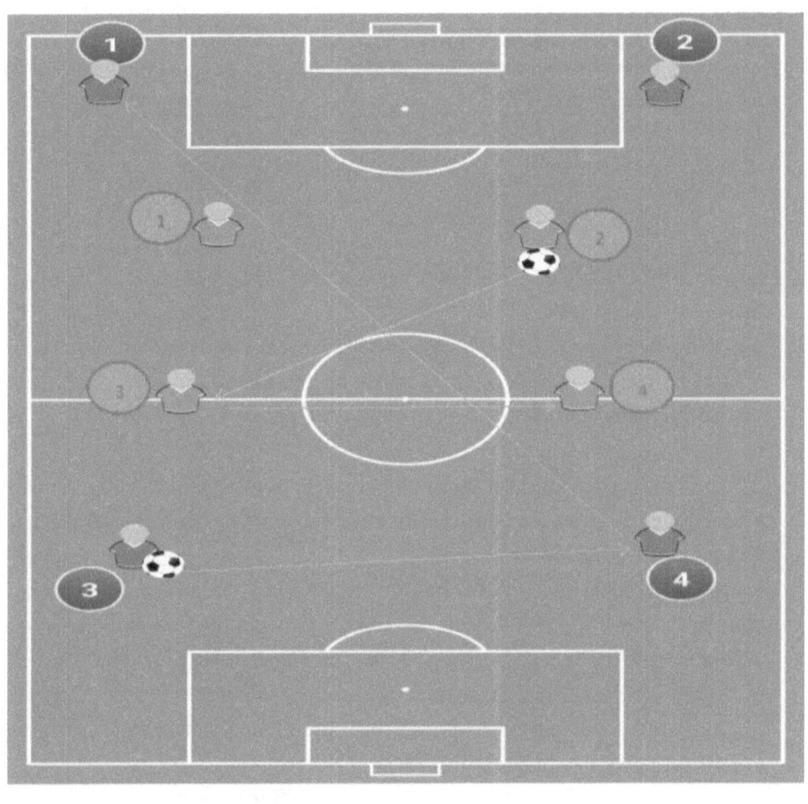

1
2

3 4

> For example in square (A) passing player after passing the ball to player no. 4 him determines the number of the player to whom player no. 4 will pass which is player no. 3.

Exercise (9)

EXERCISE NAME : CONTROL locomotive. Type of tiger : obligatory technician

The goal of the exercise : to develop players' alertness and constant concentration of attention - to develop passing with the sole of the foot

Equipment and tools : playground20*20 – colored cones – footballs – whistle

Organization and preparation : The players stand in two locomotives side by side, 10 meters apart. The control locomotive wears red and the other locomotive wears blue. The coach

places a group of colored cones in front of each locomotive in a straight line, with the same order of colors of the cones in front of the two locomotives, let it be red - yellow. - Blue - Green - White. The distance between each funnel and the other is 70 cm. The first player from the control locomotive takes possession of a soccer ball, while the first player from the blue locomotive takes possession of a soccer ball and a basketball.

Instructions : The first two players from each locomotive take turns passing footballs to each

other. The first player from the blue locomotive must dribble the basketball at the same time as the Zagzag runs between the cones, and the first player from the red locomotive must distract the first player. From the blue locomotive through his movements and running towards the cones, where it is necessary for the blue locomotive player to receive and pass next to the color of a funnel with the same color as the cone next to which the control red locomotive player is based when passing and receiving. For example, when the red locomotive player leans towards the red cone, the blue locomotive player must speed Pass the football to him while continuing to dribble the basketball, and so on, as the control locomotive player tries to distract the blue locomotive player.

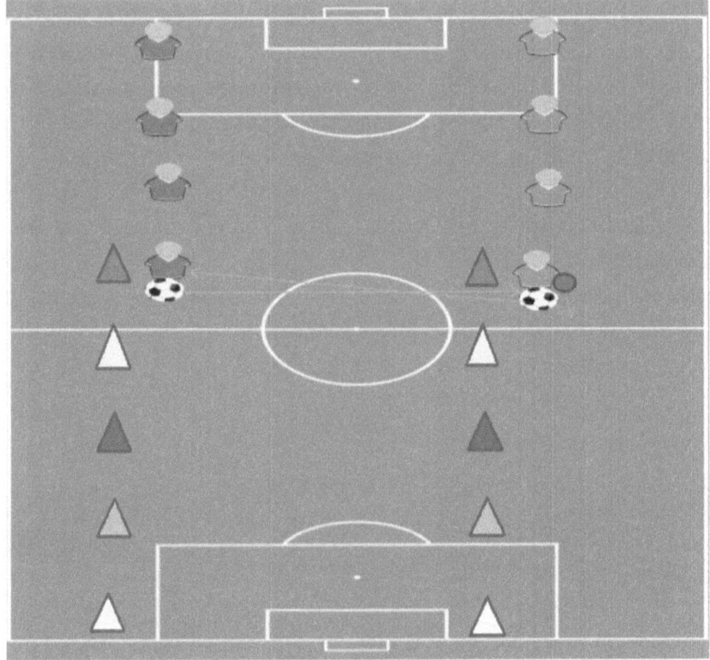

Exercise (10)

EXERCISE NAME : PASSING colors

Type of exercise : with more than one ball

The goal of the exercise : developing continuous attention and alertness for players - developing passing with the sole of the foot

Equipment and tools : football field - colored cones - football - colored players' shirts.

Organization and preparation: (8) players stand freely spread out on an area of

the court25*25 meters. Each player must wear a shirt of a different color from the other players' shirts. The shirts are as follows (red, yellow, blue, green, black, white, orange, grey). The coach places a group of colored cones with the same colors as the players' shirts freely spread across the field. The coach places a screen or phone outside the field so that the colors of the players' shirts are displayed on it randomly and at a rapid rate of time, let it be (2) seconds between each color and the other. The coach places two balls on the field, one white and the other red. We find here that the factors of the narrow space and the short time interval between the display of the colors On the screen, the large number of players, and the free movement of the players, all these stimuli require the players to continue focusing attention during the exercise.

Instructions : By alternating between passing the white ball completely freely, or the red ball,

it is passed according to the colors displayed on the screen. For example, if the screen displays a blue color, this means that the player in possession of the red ball must pass it to the player wearing blue, just as the player wearing the uniform must. The blue one, after receiving the ball, runs with it towards the blue funnel, and the players exchange passes in this way.

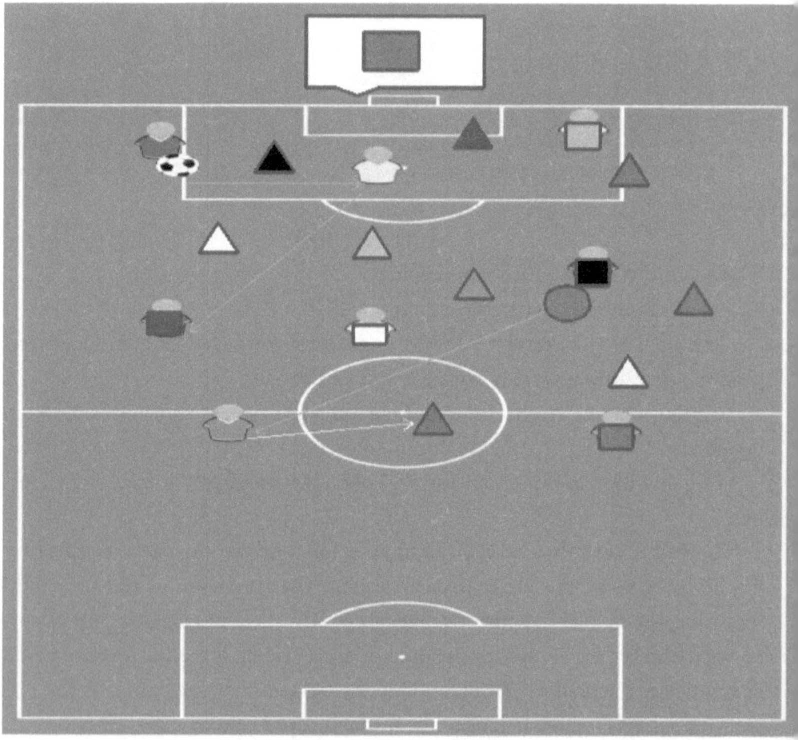

Exercise (11)

EXERCISE NAME: BALL tasks

Type of exercise: Exercise with more than one ball

The goal of the exercise: Developing players' continuous concentration of attention - Developing passing the ball with the sole of the foot

Equipment and tools: football field - numbered balls - whistle

Organization and preparation: The coach determines a field of 40 * 40 meters - divides the players into two teams, each team (7) Players, bring three footballs numbered 1:3

Instructions: At the start signal, a five-minute match is played between the two teams using

three footballs, not one ball. The team must attack with three balls and defend with three balls, and each ball must have a specific task as follows.

Ball number one is passed with the inside of the foot - Ball number two is passed with the inside of the foot -

Ball number three is passed with the outside of the foot, as the variety of tasks through an object such as the ball requires players to focus more attention.

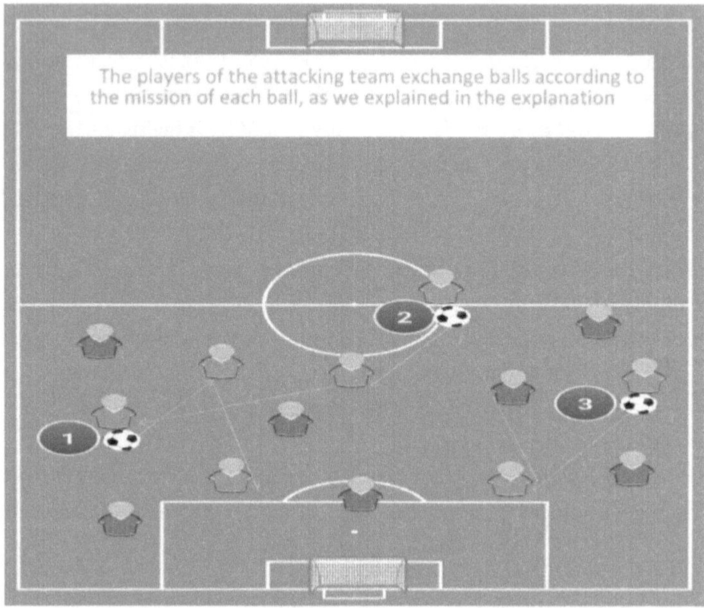

The players of the attacking team exchange balls according to the mission of each ball, as we explained in the explanation

Exercise (12) Exercise name: Scrolling through eye and head gestures

The goal of the exercise: developing the players' concentration of attention - developing passing the ball with the sole of the foot

Equipment and tools: football field - footballs - whistle

Organization and preparation: Three players each stand in the form of a triangle, with a defender in each triangle. Two base players in each triangle, each of them possessing a

soccer ball.

Instructions: At the start signal and through movement and running, the players in each triangle exchange passes to each other according to head and eye gestures. This imposes

on the players of each triangle the need to pay attention and be alert to these gestures in order to pass the ball in the correct place as the receiving player wants, for example. If the player at the head of the triangle points with his head to the right, this means that the player at the base of the triangle must pass the ball to the right of the player at the head of the triangle. Thus, the players of each triangle exchange passes between them in this way, and the defending player in the middle of the triangle must try to cut off the balls.

(Note: It is necessary for the area of the triangle to be large at the beginning of the exercise, allowing the players to find a process of alertness and concentration of attention. Over time, you can reduce that area.

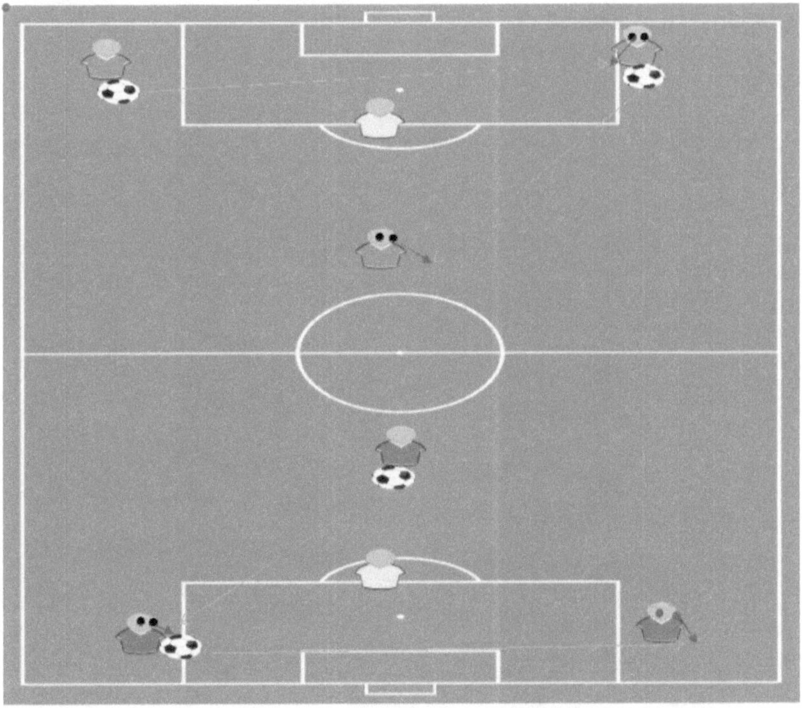

Exercise (13)

EXERCISE NAME: FAST and slow balls

The goal of the exercise: developing players' concentration of attention and alertness - developing passing with the sole of the foot

Equipment and tools: football field - footballs - whistle

Organization and preparation: The players are divided into two teams, each team has 7 players. The attacking team is in possession of two numbered balls (1:2).

Instructions: At the start signal, the attacking team attempts to pass ball number (1) Double the number of passes of the ball (2), within a specific time for the attack, let it be one minute

for the attack. This makes the players more alert and attentive to every move and pass during the attack process. The team that fails loses the attack and becomes a defender.

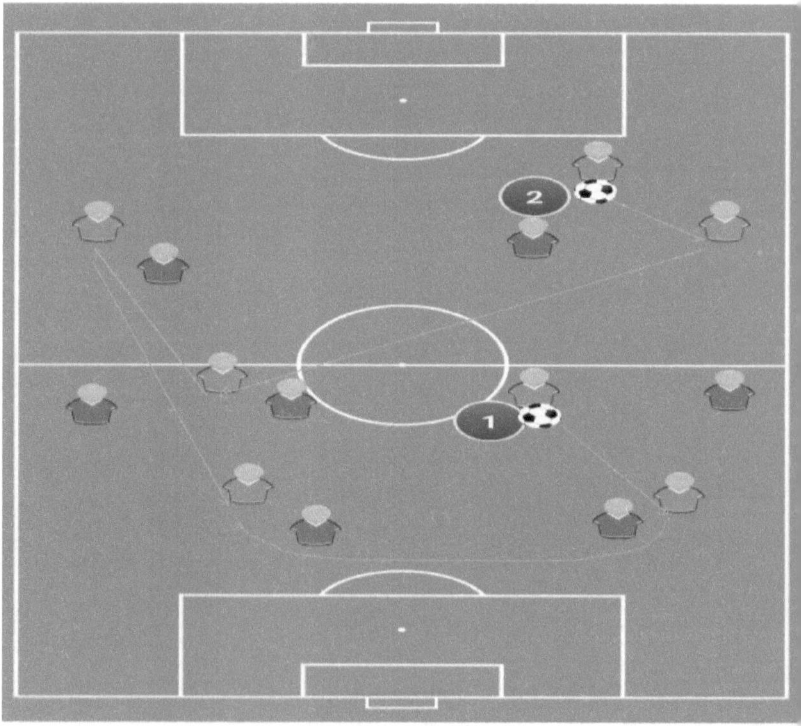

Exercise (14)

EXERCISE NAME: SHAPES of each ball

The goal of the exercise: developing players' concentration of attention and alertness - developing passing with the sole of the foot

Equipment and tools: Football field - two numbered balls (1:2) - Gear for stitching - whistle

Organization and preparation: The trainer plans geometric shapes with large areas that are

(10) meters for each geometric shape using lime (square, square minus side, circle, semicircle, rectangle minus side, trapezoid, minus side). Two numbered balls (1:2) are prepared, and the players are divided into two teams, each team has (7) players. .

Instructions: The attacking team passes ball number (1) Through complete geometric shapes, and passes ball number (2) through the incomplete geometric shapes. If the

attacking team makes mistakes on one of the two balls, the attack is lost. Such a performance requires each player to pay attention to the movements of teammates and competitors on the field, which requires vigilance and focused attention for the players. .

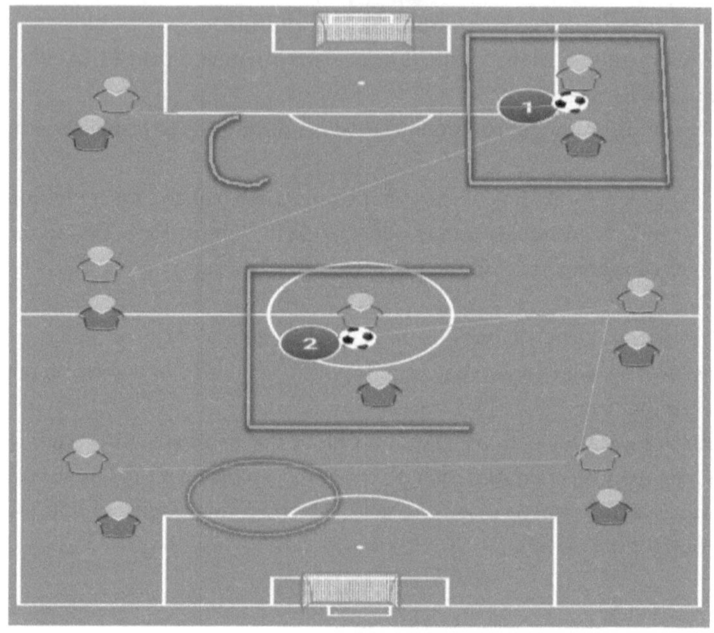

Exercise (15)

Exercise name: Three steps running Exercise type: mini game

The goal of the exercise: developing the alertness and concentration of the players' attention

- developing the sense of the ball

Equipment and tools: football field - footballs - cones

Organization and preparation: standing (6) Of the players in a free spread on a 25*25 m field, each player in possession of the ball, with two defenders present.

Instructions: At the start signal, each of the players in possession of the balls runs with the ball three steps, then passes to one of his teammates in possession of the balls, while the

defenders try to cut off the balls from the players in possession. To increase the difficulty of the exercise, a third defender can be added.

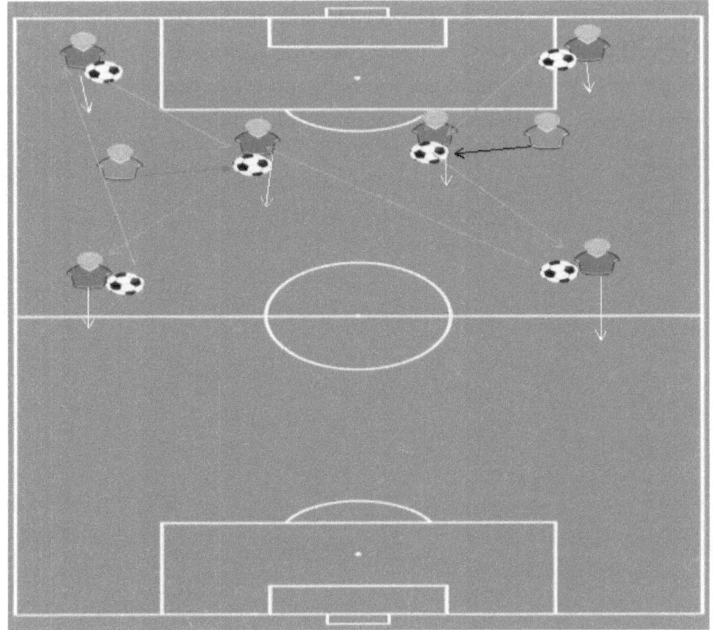

Exercise (16)

EXERCISE NAME: MINDFULNESS Ladder

Type of exercise: Training on basic skills linked to physical attributes

The goal of the exercise: developing vigilance and constant attention to players - developing passing with the sole of the foot

Tools and equipment: football field - agility ladders - footballs - whistle

Organization and preparation: The players are divided into two adjacent trains (A) With a ball

(B) Without a ball, the distance between them is ten meters. The first player from the locomotive (A) takes possession of a soccer ball. In front of each locomotive is an agility ladder. Five meters after the end of the stairs, a player stands in the middle, possessing a handball.

Instructions: At the start signal, the first player from each locomotive starts running on the

agility ladder, if the middle player passes the handball to the locomotive player (B) This means that the locomotive player (A) must pass the ball to the midfield player. However, if the midfield player passes the ball to the locomotive player (A), this means that the player must pass the football to the locomotive player (B). Thus, the players exchange passes until the end of the ladder, where The last player in possession of the football passes it to the second player in the locomotive (A) And so the performance continues .

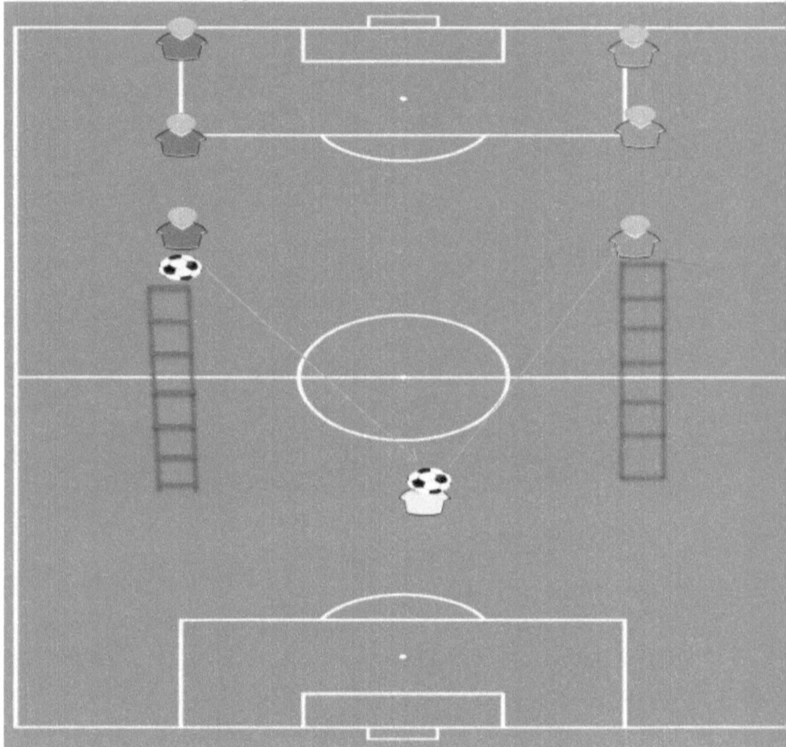

Exercise (17)

Exercise name: Control locomotive

Type of exercise: Training on basic skills while linking them to physical attributes

The goal of the exercise: developing players' continuous focus of attention - developing passing with the sole of the foot

Organization and preparation: The players are divided into two adjacent locomotives, ten meters apart. Each player takes possession of the locomotive (A) On a soccer ball,

locomotive players (B) without balls. Colored cones are placed in front of each locomotive. The distance between each cone is 50 cm. The colors of the cones are as follows (red, yellow, blue, and green). The arrangement of the cones is identical for both locomotives.

Instructions: At the start signal, the first player from each locomotive starts a zigzag run from between the cones, if the locomotive player stops (B) who does not possess a ball next to

the cone on the locomotive player ((A) who has possession of the ball passes to him from the side of the cone of the same color as the cone next to which the player stands, and thus the players exchange passes until the end of the cone, then each player returns to the end of his locomotive to start the second player from each Locomotive by repeating the performance and so on.

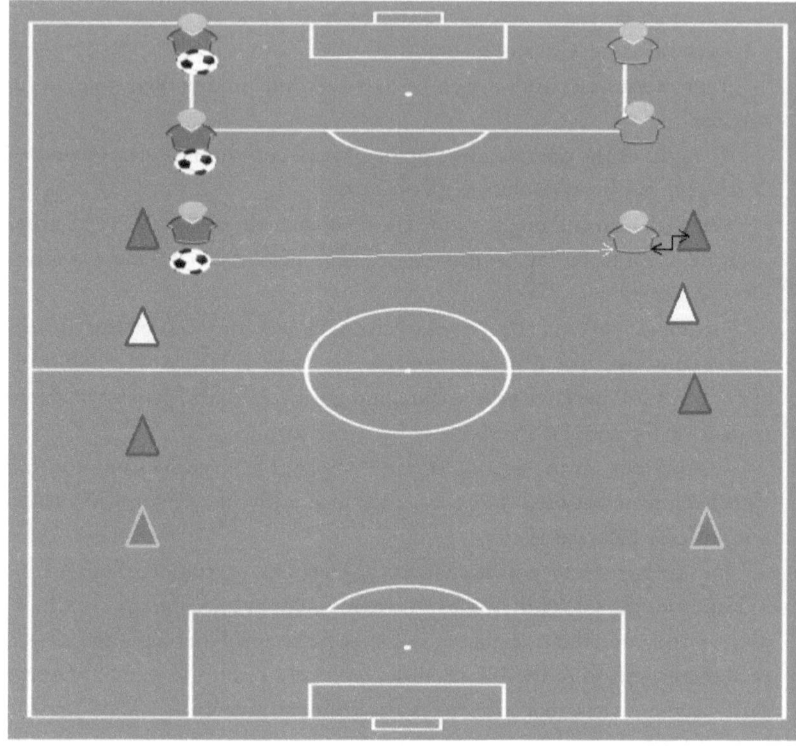

Exercise (18)

EXERCISE NAME: (10) Passes Exercise type: mini-game

The goal of the exercise: developing the players' concentration of attention - developing passing the ball with the sole of the foot

Equipment and tools: playground30*30 m – football – whistle.

Organization and preparation: The coach divides the players into two teams, each of which6) Players - You must play a football match between them, lasting 5 minutes.

Instructions: At the start signal, the attacking team attempts to end the attack by (10) Passes or less - The team that cannot finish the attack within ten passes loses the ball and becomes

a defender. Likewise, if the ball is cut off from it, it becomes a defender. This requires the players to focus more attention in order to effectively pass to end the attack with an appropriate number of passes.

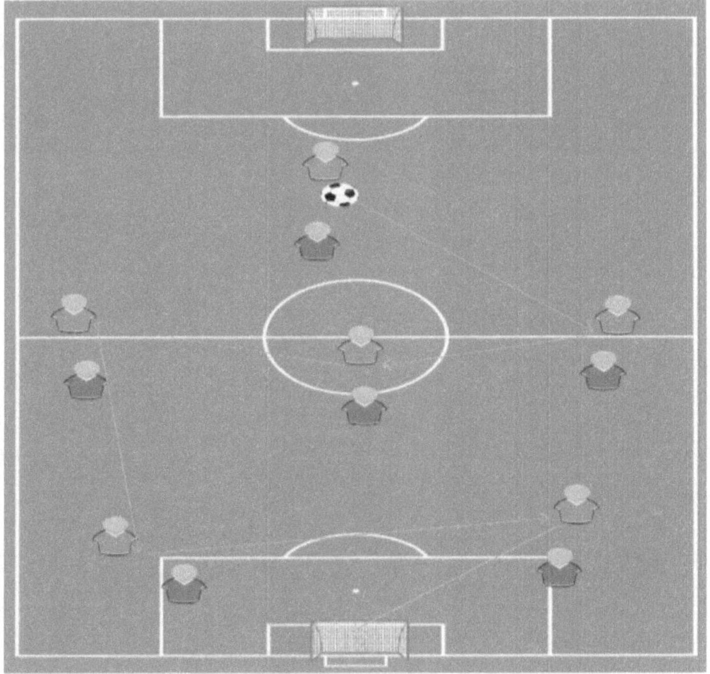

Exercise (19)

EXERCISE NAME: INDIVIDUAL - Doubles Exercise type: mini games

The goal of the exercise: to develop players' alertness and concentration - to develop passing with the sole of the foot

Equipment and tools: football field - soccer ball - whistle

Organization and preparation: The players are divided into two teams of (7) players each, with each team wearing a uniform numbered from (1:7).

Instructions: At the start signal, the players of the attacking team exchange passes among themselves, with each player passing in the opposite direction to the type of shirt number he

is wearing. For example, if the number one player wants to pass, he must pass to a player wearing an even type shirt, and vice versa for players who wear shirts bearing numbers.

Even players must pass to players wearing odd-numbered jerseys

> **Each player on the attacking team passes against the shirt number he or she is wearing.**

Exercise (20) Exercise name: Forced longitudinal pass

Exercise type: mini games

The goal of the exercise: developing the alertness and concentration of the players' attention

- developing passing with the sole of the foot.

Equipment and tools: football field - soccer ball - whistle.

Organization and preparation: The players are divided into two teams, each team has (7) players + a goalkeeper.

A 5-minute match is held between them.

Instructions: The attacking team must not pass more than three consecutive balls crosswise, as it is necessary for the players to pay attention to the longitudinal pass that cuts spaces towards the opposing team. The team that passes more than three consecutive passes

crosswise or from which the ball is cut becomes a defender and a goal is counted against it. What imposes on the players the necessity of positive passing, which will only come by focusing attention on every move and pass so that this can be done.

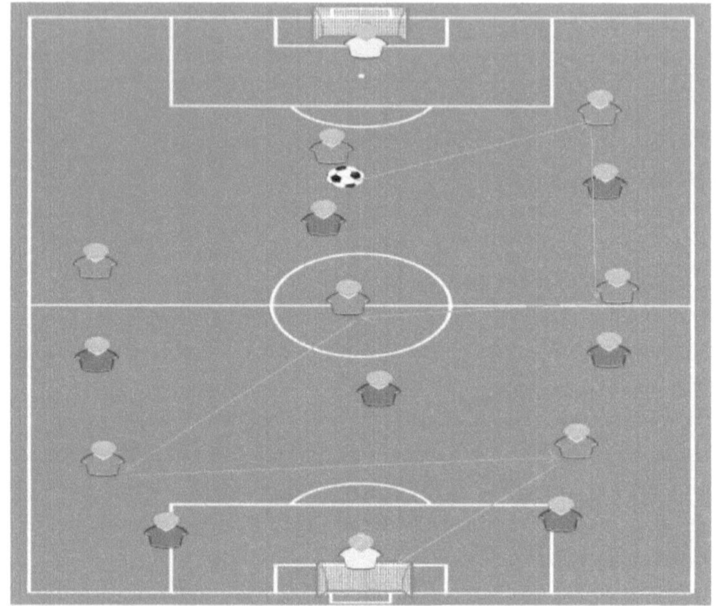

the exercise (21)

EXERCISE NAME: RUNNING with the ball, more than three steps in pairs - less than three steps in singles.

The goal of the exercise: to develop players' alertness and concentration - to develop passing with the sole of the foot

Equipment and tools: football field - numbered uniforms for each team - football - whistle.

Organization and preparation: The players are divided into two teams and a 5-minute match is played between them.

Instructions: The attacking team's player passes to end the attack as follows

If one of the players runs with the ball more than three steps, he passes the ball to a player wearing an even shirt - but if the number of steps is less than three steps, he passes it to a player wearing an odd shirt, and so on until the attack ends. The player who makes a mistake loses the ball to his team and becomes a defender.

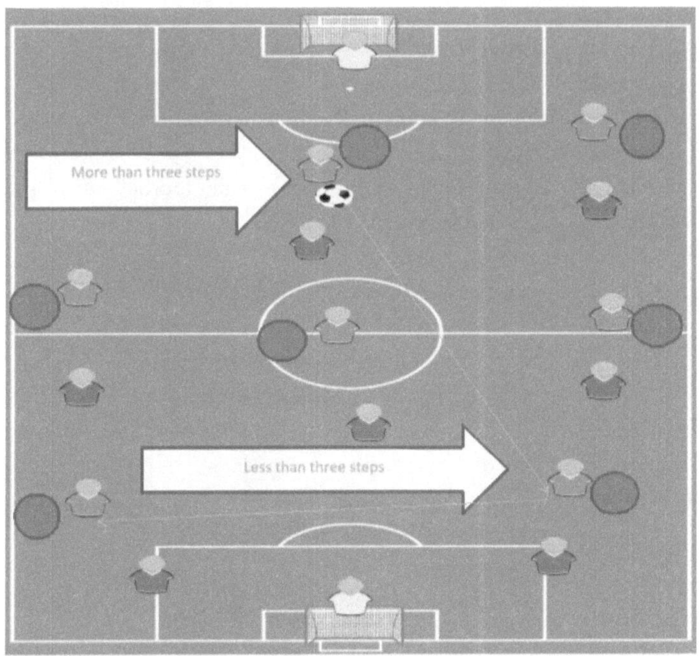

1 2
More than three steps

5
3
4

Less than three steps

6
7

Examples of exercises to develop divided attention through basic skils training methods

EXERCISE (1) EXERCISE name: Wall and screen numbers.

Type of exercise: ball sensation exercise.

The goal of the exercise: developing the divided attention of the players - developing the sense of the ball.

Equipment and tools: football field - stadium wall - football - display screen.

Organization and preparation: The trainer places a screen on a wall so that it displays the numbers from

(1:10) randomly at a rate of two seconds between switching numbers on the screen, then the trainer draws circles or squares numbered from (10:1) randomly in the lower center of the wall at the bottom of the screen. The learner player stands facing the wall at a distance of ten meters, holding a ball. foot

Instructions: At the start signal, the learning player passes the ball forcefully to the number of the square that is displayed on the screen, and this performance continues for a minute, then the second player, and so on until the team finishes.

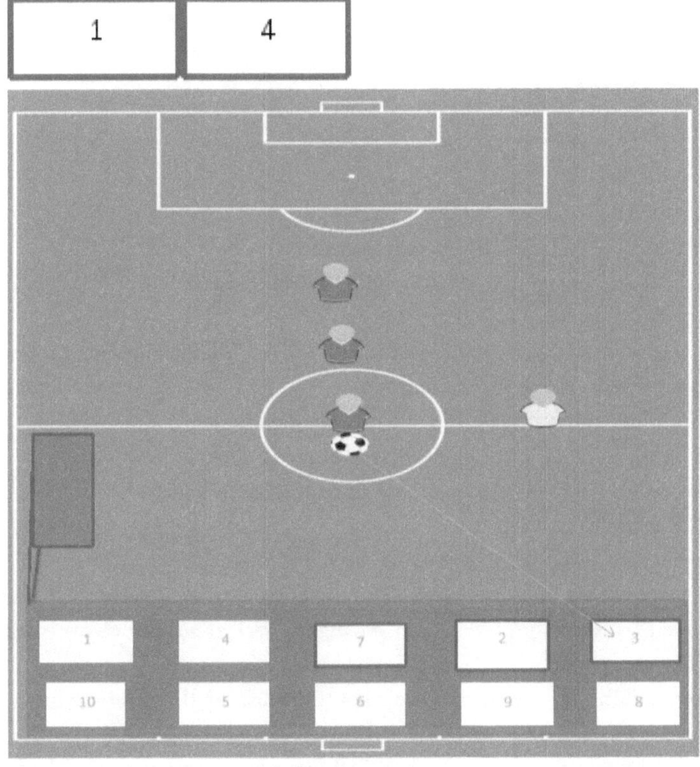

7 2 3

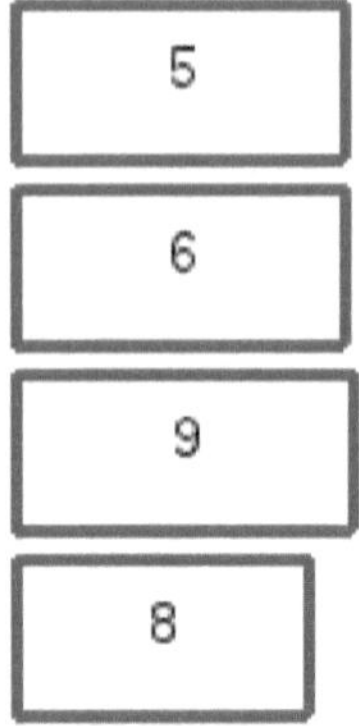

Exercise (2)

EXERCISE NAME: SCREEN numbers and laser guidance, physical.

Exercise type: Training in basic skills while linking them to physical attributes.

The goal of the exercise: developing the players' divided attention - developing passing with the sole of the foot.

Equipment and tools: football field - stadium wall - football - display screen - laser lighting. Organization and preparation: The coach installs a screen on the wall at the level of the learner's head and eyes so that it displays the numbers from (1:10) Randomly at a rate of

two seconds between switching numbers on the screen, then the coach draws circles or squares in the middle of the bottom of the wall at the bottom of the screen. The learner player stands facing the wall at a distance of ten meters, holding a soccer ball.

Instructions: The learner player takes turns passing the ball forcefully across the squares on

the wall according to the coach directing the laser towards one of the squares on the wall, with the player mentioning the order of the numbers that are displayed on this display screen while the player is running cross-court between the cones. This performance makes the player deal with A fixed stimulus and a sudden moving stimulus represented by the difference in directing the laser by the coach toward a different square every time a new number is displayed on the screen during skill and physical performance, which increases the difficulty of dividing the player's attention while performing the exercise.

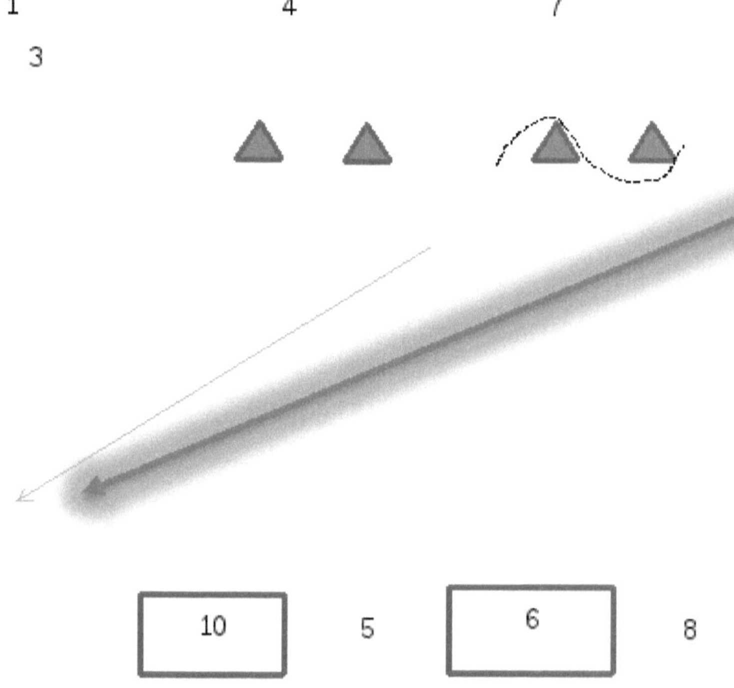
1
3
4
7
10
5
6
8

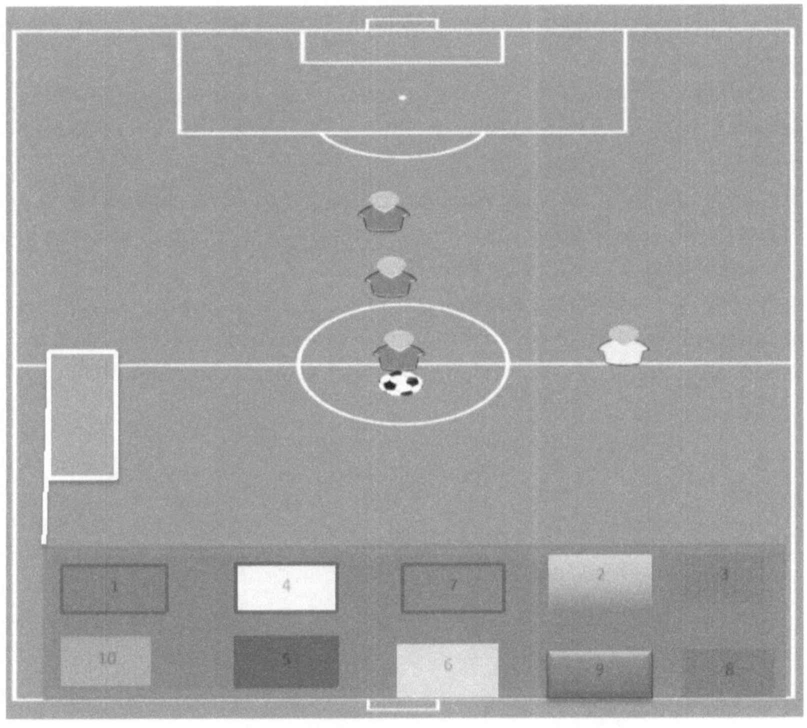

9

Exercise (3)

Exercise name: Similar squares

The goal of the exercise: developing the divided attention of the players - developing the sense of the ball.

Type of exercise: ball sensation exercise. Equipment and tools: football field - cones - footballs

Organization and preparation: The coach identifies two adjacent fields, each with an area of

\u200b\u200btheir area20 * 20 m

The players are divided into two groups, each group consisting of (4) players wearing numbered shirts

((4: 1 Group (A) in blue inside the first square, Group (B) in red inside the second square - each player in both groups takes possession of a soccer ball.

Instructions: At the start signal, each player from the group stands upA)) performs any

feeling exercises that come to his mind from running inside his own box, provided that performing one exercise does not last more than ten seconds. At the same time, each player from group B)) performs the same performance as the player with the same jersey number from the group. (B) After three minutes, the two groups switch roles. In this exercise, the player must divide attention between the performance he is performing and the performance performed by the player with the same shirt number in the other square. This requires the players to have more ability to divide attention in terms of performance. Free movement and spread makes it more difficult for the player to divide the attention.

1
3
2
4

3

2
1

4

Exercise (4)

EXERCISE NAME: FOOTBALL - Basketball. Type of exercise: ball sensation exercise.

The goal of the exercise: developing the divided attention of the players - developing the sense of the ball.

Equipment and tools: football field - soccer balls - basketballs.

Organization and preparation: The players stand freely spread across the court. Each player has a basketball in his hand and a soccer ball in front of his foot.

Instructions: At the start signal, each player alternates passing the football between the right and left feet and dribbling the basketball.

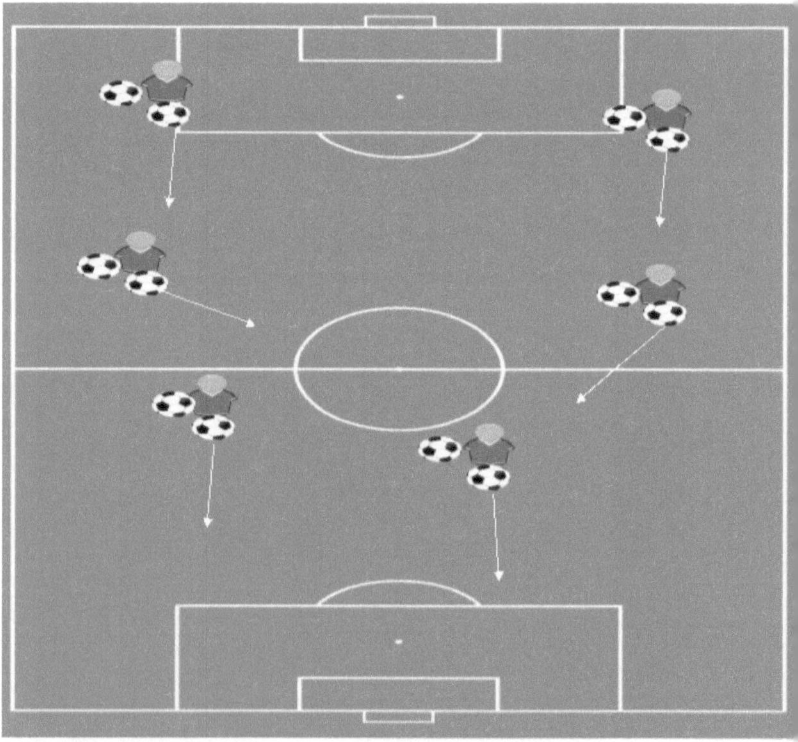

EXERCISE (5) EXERCISE name: Basketball, running, passing.

Exercise type: Training in basic skills while linking them to physical attributes.

The goal of the exercise: to develop the players' divided attention - passing with the sole of the foot.

Equipment and tools: football field - soccer balls - basketballs.

Organization and preparation: The players are divided into two adjacent trains, with a distance of ten meters between them. The first player from each train takes possession of a football and a basketball. In front of each train is a group of cones with identical colors for

both groups.

Instructions: At the start signal, the first player from each locomotive runs with a football and dribbles a basketball, with both players taking turns passing footballs to each other.

Exercise (6) Exercise name: Chasing the cunning fox

Exercise type: feeling the ball

The goal of the exercise: developing the divided attention of the players - developing the feeling of the ball

Equipment and tools: football field - footballs - colored cones

Organization and preparation: The players stand in a free spread on the field. Each player is in possession of a football. The coach places a group of colored cones in a free spread on the field. There is a joker player on the field (the cunning fox).

Instructions: Players chase the joker while maintaining the performance as follows

If the joker player stands next to the red funnel, the players bounce the ball on his foot while moving towards him to chase him. If he stands next to the blue funnel, they alternate passing the ball between the feet while moving towards him. If he stands next to the yellow funnel, they pull the ball under the foot while moving towards him.

The Joker's mission is to distract the players during the performance.

We notice here that when the joker is standing nest to
the yellow funnel, the foot while running towards him to
chase him

We notice here that when the joker is standing nest to the yellow funnel, the foot while running towards him to chase him

Exercise (7)

Exercise name: Colored squares

The goal of the exercise: developing divided attention - developing a sense of the ball

Equipment and tools: football field - numbered cones - whistle

Organization and preparation: The trainer determines (4) Small squares, each square

measuring 5*5 m. At each square, two players stand facing each other: a joker without a ball and a learner player with a soccer ball.

Instructions: At the start signal, the learner player chases the joker player while paying attention to the joker player's movements. If the joker player is stationed next to the red

funnel, the learner player must chase him by exchanging passes of the ball between the feet. If the joker player is stationed next to the yellow funnel, the learner player must chase him through Drawing the ball with the bottom of the foot, and if the joker player rests next to the blue funnel, he chases it by running with the ball with the front side of the foot.

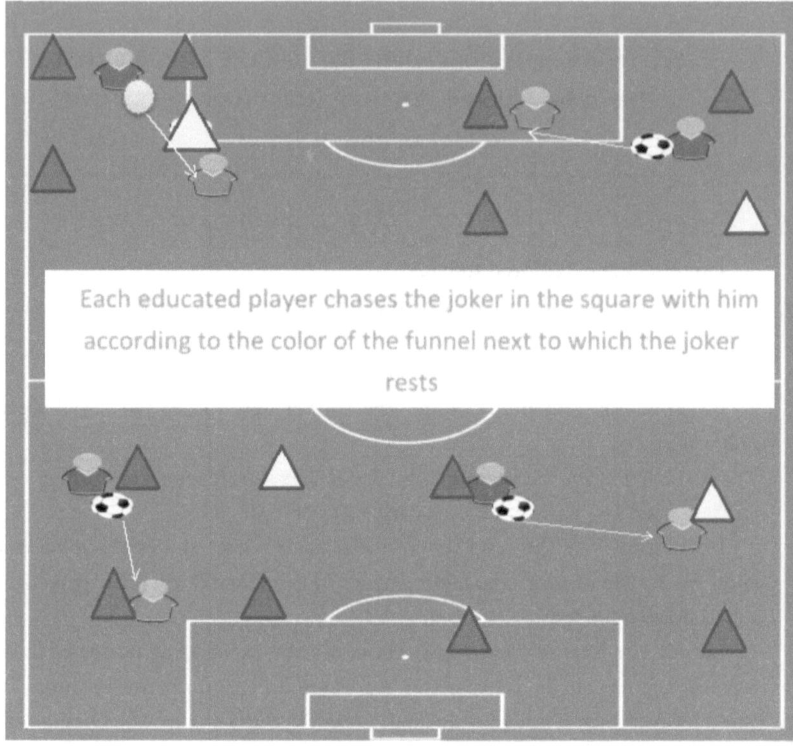

Each educated player chases the joker in the square with him
according to the color of the funnel next to which the joker
rests

> Each educated player chases the joker in the square with him according to the color of the funnel next to which the joker rests

Exercise (8)

Exercise name: Swapping numbers

Type of exercise: Complex physical skill exercise

The goal of the exercise: developing divided attention - developing a sense of the ball

Equipment and tools: football field - footballs - whistle

Organization and preparation: The players are divided into two squares. The first has players wearing blue shirts numbered (1:4), and the second square has players wearing red

and with the same numbered shirts. Each square takes possession of one soccer ball. Outside the two squares, two players stand facing each other. One of them takes possession of a soccer ball, and one of them also takes possession of a soccer ball. On numbered cards(1:4) in blue and the other player holds the same numbers of cards in red, with a defender inside each square.

Instructions: At the start signal, the players of each square, as well as the two players facing each other, alternate passing the ball with the soles of their feet. The players of each square

must pay attention to the player who carries cards of the same color as the shirt they are wearing. If he raises his card number, let it be a single number, it is necessary for the player to run number one into the square. In order for them to exchange positions together, it is necessary for the movements of the two players facing each other outside the square to be varied and quick. This forces the players of each square to have more divided attention.

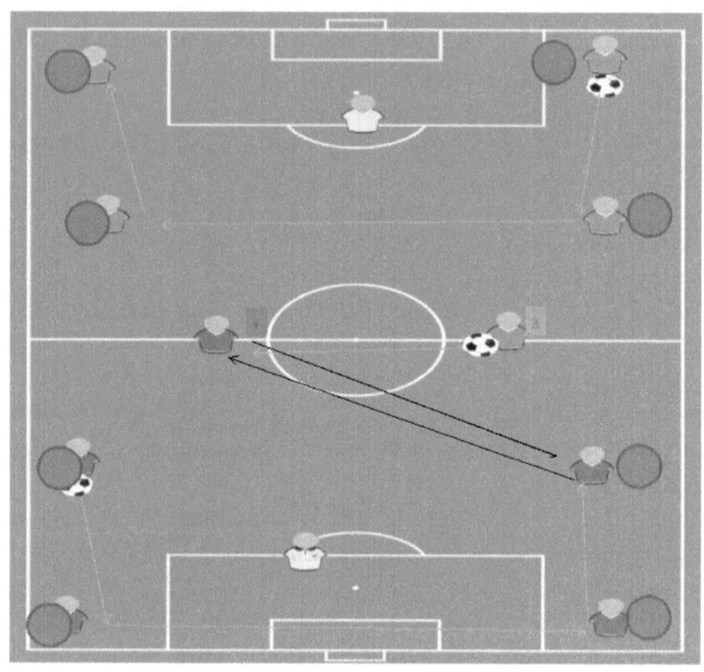

4 1

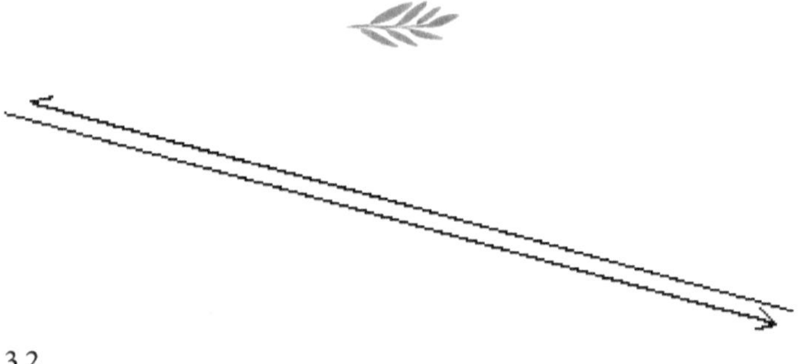

3 2

1

3

4 1

3 2

EXERCISE (9) EXERCISE name: Match the order of the players

Type of exercise: Compound physical exercise

The goal of the exercise: to develop passing with the sole of the foot - to develop the players' divided attention

Equipment and tools: football field - footballs - whistle

Organization and preparation: The players stand in three rows in a row, with the distance between each row being ten metres, and the arrangement of the players in each row in a row is (1:5)

Each player in the first row has possession of a soccer ball, the players in the middle row and the players in the last row without a ball

Instructions: At the start signal, the first-row players exchange passes with the second-row players. The task of the third-row players is to switch positions among themselves in order to

force the first- and second-row players to change their positions in the same order as the third-row players with each pass. This is what is imposed on the first-row players. The second is division of attention

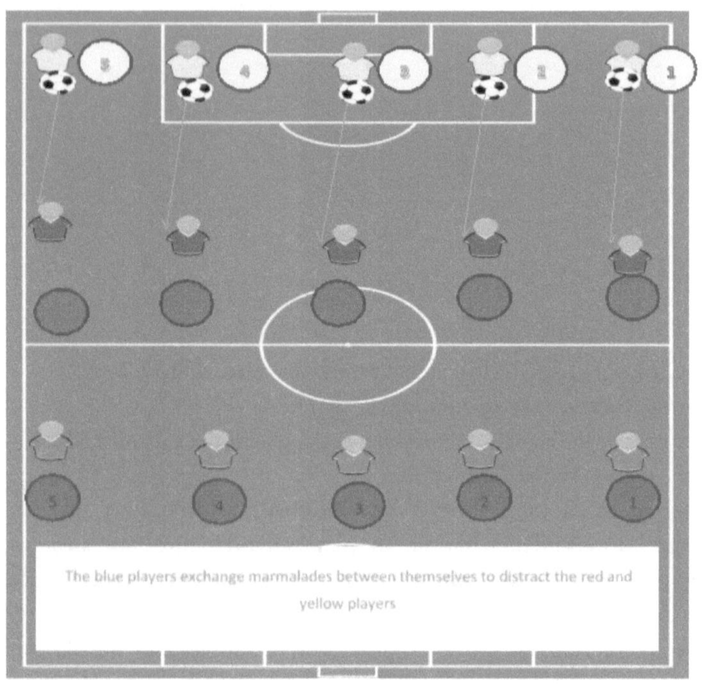

5 4 3 2 1

5 4 3 2 1

Exercise (10)

EXERCISE NAME: SIGNAL box

The goal of the exercise: developing divided attention - developing passing with the sole of the foot

Type of exercise: Mandatory technical exercise Equipment and tools: football field - soccer ball - whistle

Organization and preparation: standing (4) Players in a square formation must wear numbered shirts

(1 : 4) Someone grabs a soccer ball

Instructions: The ball is passed between them through signals. When the player in possession of the ball passes, the task of the other players is to distract the player as

follows. If the passing player is wearing a number one shirt, he passes to the player who is pointing with his hand, number two, even if he is not wearing a number two shirt. Shirt number two, where the passing is in ascending order from (1:4), and this depends on the players' signals and not the shirt numbers they are wearing. Likewise, where the passing depends on the players' signals, it is necessary for all players to point to different numbers when the player in possession of the ball tries to pass in order to disperse the ball. Attention: If more than one player points with the same number with his hand, the player in possession must pass to him. Here, the passer must pass to the player wearing the shirt number closest in number. That is, if one is the passer and two, three, and four point with the number 2, then here player number one passes to the player. Number two is considered the closest in number, and thus the players exchange passes.

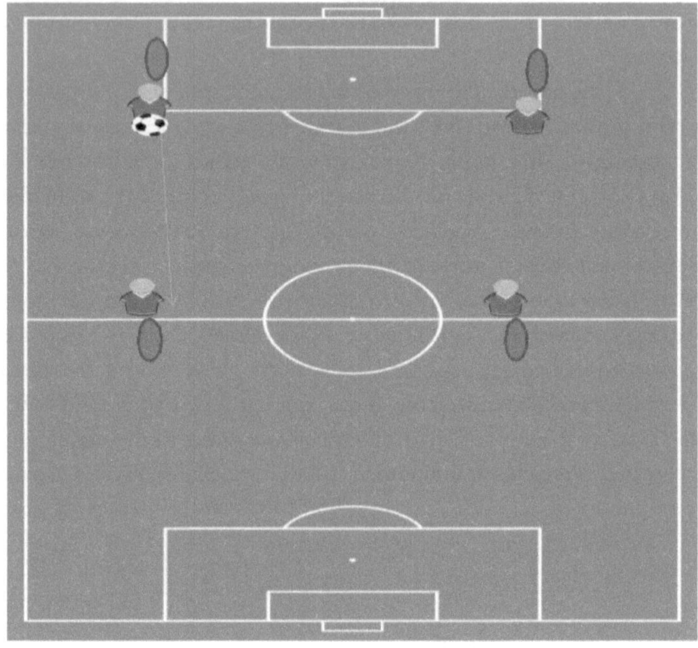

2
1

4

43

Exercise (11)

THE SAME EXERCISE AS before, with a defender in the middle of the square trying to extract the ball from the players, which requires the players to divide their attention more

Exercise (12)

EXERCISE NAME: WHERE is the ball?

Type of exercise: Mandatory technical exercise

The goal of the exercise: developing the players' divided attention - developing the performance of passing with the sole of the foot

Equipment and tools: football field - footballs - whistle

Organization and preparation: The trainer determines two squares facing each other, the area of each square20*20 m

Centered on the sides of each square (4) Players numbered from (1:4), in each square there is one soccer ball

Instructions: At the start signal, the players of each square exchange passes with the sole of

the foot among themselves, provided that the player in possession of the ball in each square remembers the location of the ball in the other square. For example, when player number one in the first square is in possession of the ball, it is necessary before He passes to one of his teammates and states out loud whether the ball in the second square is with any of the players. The players in the second square do the same while passing the ball with the sole of the foot to each other.

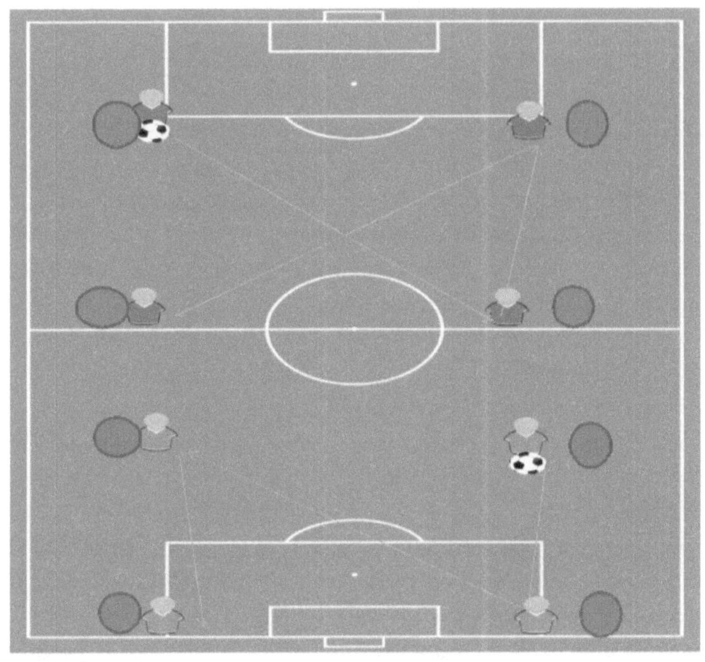

21

34

14

23

Exercise (13)

THE SAME EXERCISE AS before, there is a defender in the middle of each square trying to extract the ball from the players, which forces the players of each square to divide more attention between more than one stimulus.

This also requires more division of attention

Exercise (14) Exercise name: 6 against 2 with more than one ball Type of exercise: Exercise with more than one ball

The goal of the exercise: Developing players' divided attention - developing passing with the sole of the foot

Tools and equipment: 25 * 25 m field - footballs - whistle

Organization and preparation: The players are divided into (6) attackers and (2) defenders on a 25 * 25 court.M In a free spread, each of the attackers has possession of a soccer ball.

Instructions: At the start signal, the attacking players exchange balls among themselves, while the defenders try to extract the balls. This makes the players pay attention to more

than one stimulus at the same time.

Exercise (15)

EXERCISE NAME: CONTROL square

The goal of the exercise: Developing players' divided attention - developing passing with the sole of the foot

Equipment and tools: football field - numbered cones - numbered footballs – whistle

Organization and preparation: The players are divided into two squares. The first square

represents the control group for performance - The second square represents the experimental group. Each square has two balls numbered respectively (2,1). Outside each square there is a group of cones numbered (2,1) as well.

Instructions: At the start signal, the players of each square exchange passes between them,

provided that the players of the control square move and position themselves on the cones outside the square, so that passing one ball is within the borders of the square and the second is outside the borders of the square, in an attempt to distract the attention of the players of the experimental square, who are required to repeat and do the same thing. The performance performed by the players of the control square, whereby if the players of the control square, through one of them moving outside the boundaries of the square and positioning himself next to a certain numbered cone, pass the ball number one outside the square, for example, the players of the experimental square perform the same performance. This requires speed and accuracy of division. Attention

1

2

1

2

Exercise (16)

EXERCISE NAME: SHADED rectangle

Type of exercise: exercise with more than one ball

The goal of the exercise : is to develop the players' divided attention - to develop passing with the sole of the foot

Tools and equipment: 25 * 25 m field - footballs - pitch planning equipment - whistle

Organization and preparation: The coach plans the field into two equal squares separated by a shaded rectangle three meters wide. Each square contains four players wearing uniforms numbered from one to four, each player in possession of a ball.

Instructions: The players of each square exchange passes to each other, with the players of each square trying to deceive the other square. This is as follows: If a player enters the

shaded rectangle separating the two squares, it is necessary for the player who wears the same shirt number in the other square to exchange passes with him. The player who does not notice this. Within three seconds he switches roles with the defender in his own box

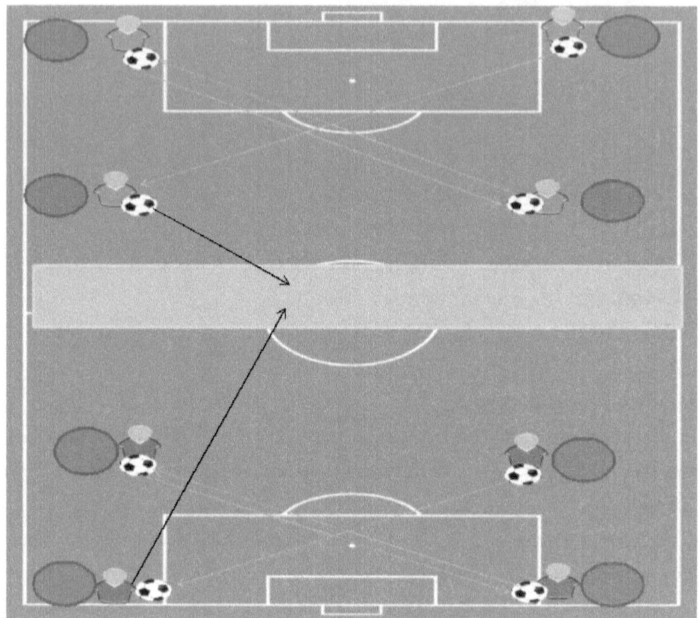

2 1

3 4

4 1

3 2

Exercise (17)

THE SAME EXERCISE AS before, with a defender in each square trying to extract the balls, which requires the players to divide attention more between more than one stimulus. The exercise can be made more difficult by narrowing the area of the square in which each group is based. It is also possible to narrow a square and the second square remains as it is. What requires the players of the smaller square to be more focused and divide attention due to the ability of the large square group to work easily and quickly, which puts the players of the smaller square under real pressure similar to playing situations in matches.

Exercise (18) Exercise name: Pay attention to the joker

Type of exercise: Training on basic skills linked to physical attributes

The goal of the exercise: Developing players' divided attention - developing passing with the sole of the foot

Tools and equipment: half a football field - balls, colored cones

Organization and preparation: The players stand as two locomotives.A) The touchline area on the right side in the red uniform, the locomotive (B) The touchline area on the left side in the blue uniform.

Each player from the two locomotives has possession of a ball. The coach places a group of blue and red colored cones in front of each locomotive, at unequal distances. A joker player stands in the space between the two locomotives, holding two blue and red cards in his hand.

Instructions: At the start signal, the first player from each locomotive starts running with the

ball, paying attention to the signal of the joker player. If he points the red card, this means that the first player from the locomotive must (A) The one wearing the red uniform passes the ball to the joker player. As for the first player from the locomotive (b), he stands next to the nearest red funnel. At the moment when the joker receives the ball, he has two options to distract the players. Either he passes the ball back to the player to whom he passed it, or He passes to the locomotive player (B), and this forces the player to pass the ball in his possession to the continent player (A) before the ball coming from the joker reaches him, and so the performance is repeated.

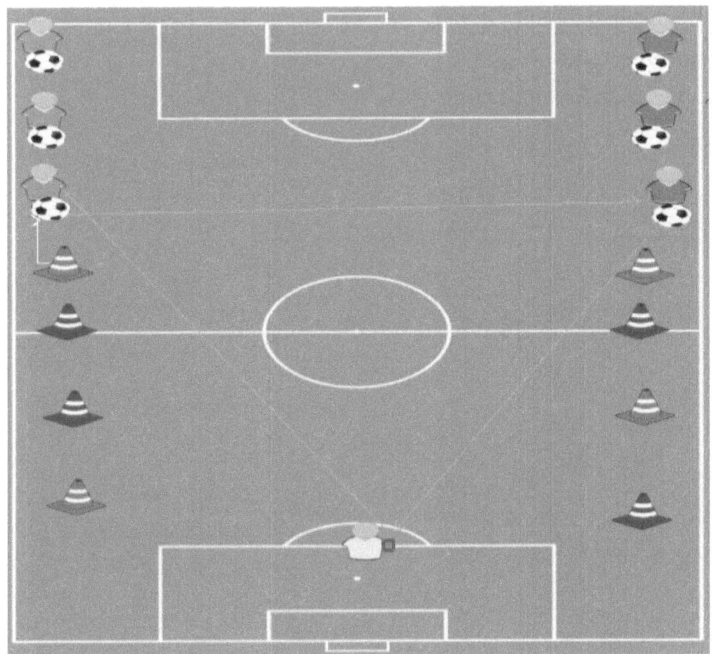

Exercise (19)

EXERCISE NAME: TEAM signals Exercise type: mini game

The goal of the exercise: Developing players' divided attention - developing passing with the sole of the foot

Tools and equipment: soccer field - soccer ball - whistle

Organization and preparation: The coach determines the court area25 * 25 m, the players are divided into two teams, each team

(7) Players of one team wear red uniforms and the other team wears blue uniforms. The coach gives the captain of each team a sheet of paper before the match on which are written five signals used by two players from the team. For example, the signals can be numbers. For example, the red team uses 1, 3, 5. 7,9 are used as their signals to distract the player in possession of the ball on the attacking team, while the blue team uses 2,4,6,8,10 as their signals.

Instructions: Signals are used in each team by only two players determined by the captain of each team. When the attacking player in possession of the ball is unable to see and say the

two signals out loud, his team loses the ball. If he is able to see and say one signal, his team

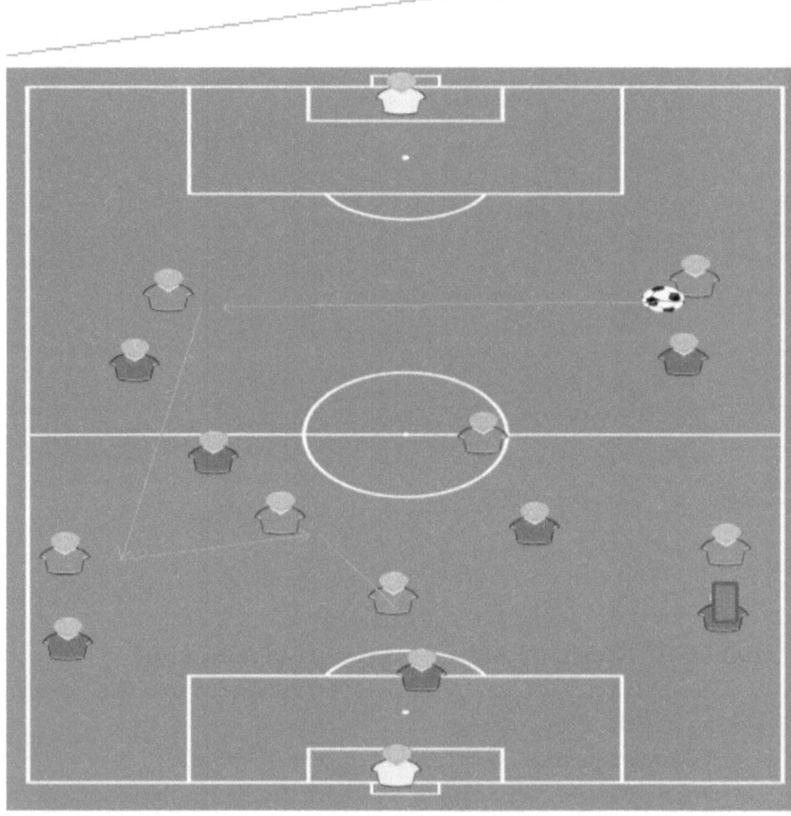

is given thirty seconds to finish the attack through passing, if not. The team succeeds. During this period, the team becomes a defender

Exercise (19)

EXERCISE NAME: FOOT and hand Exercise type: mini game

The goal of the exercise: Developing players' divided attention - developing passing with the sole of the foot

Tools and equipment: football field - soccer ball - handball - whistle - goal for each team Organization and preparation: The players are divided into two teams, red and blue, each team has 7 players. The attacking team takes possession of two soccer balls and a

handball.

Instructions: At the start signal, one player on the attacking team takes possession of a football and another player takes possession of a handball. The attacking team performs as

follows: If the player in possession of the football passes to a player wearing an odd- numbered uniform, the other player in possession of the handball passes the handball to another player. He wears an even number and vice versa. This is how the performance takes place between team members until reaching the defending team's goal and ending the attack. If the attacking team makes mistakes by passing in this way or the defending team recovers the ball, the attacking team becomes a defender.

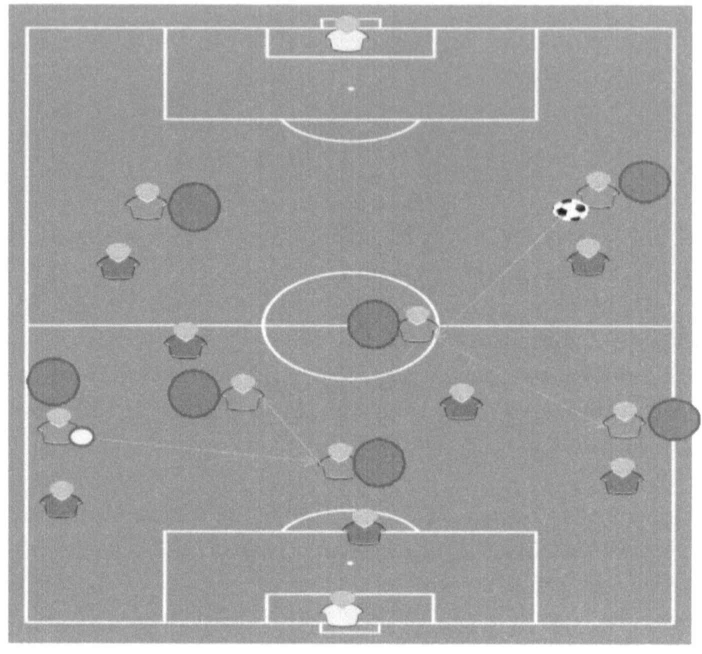

1
5

3

2
7
6

4

Exercise (20)
Exercise name: Reverse lane Exercise type: mini game
The goal of the exercise: Developing players' divided attention
- developing passing with the sole of the foot

Tools and equipment: soccer field - soccer ball - whistle

Organization and preparation: The players are divided into two teams, each team has (7) players, one team in the red numbered uniform and the other in the blue numbered uniform. A five-minute match is held between the two

teams.

Instructions: The team in possession of the ball must exchange passes as follows: When the player in possession passes the ball to one of his teammates

with his right foot, the team receiving the ball passes to one of his teammates with his left foot to a player wearing an individual shirt, and when the player in possession of the ball passes with his left foot, the player receiving the ball passes with his foot. The Yemeni player is wearing my husband's shirt.

Technical points: Focus on the technical points of passing with the sole of the foot

Here, when player number one passed the ball with his right foot m player number two passed it with his left foot to a player wearing an individual shirt

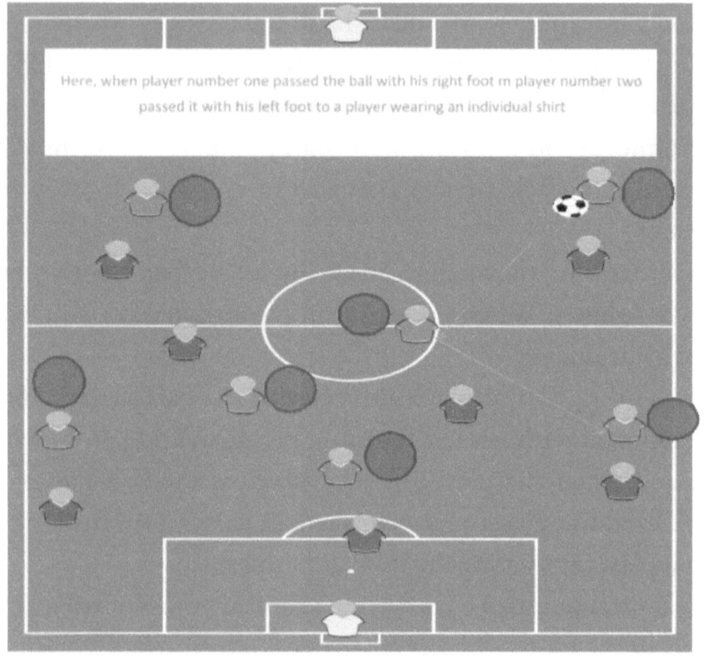

41

2

7 5

3

6

EXERCISE (1) EXERCISE name: Choosing task numbers

Type of exercise: ball sensation exercise

The goal of the exercise: developing selective attention for players - developing passing with the sole of the foot

Tools and equipment: football field - display screen or telephone - footballs Organization and preparation: The players stand in a row or freely spread out on the field in front of a telephone or a display screen that the coach installs at

a suitable height on the field. Geometric shapes are randomly displayed on the screen, each shape containing a group of numbers.

Instructions: The players' task is to pay attention to the numbers inside each

geometric shape. If they find the number (1), the players dribble the ball with their right foot from moving and walking, and if they find the number (2), they alternate passing the ball between the feet, right and left, from running. If they find Number three take turns touching the ball with the bottom of their feet from a standstill.

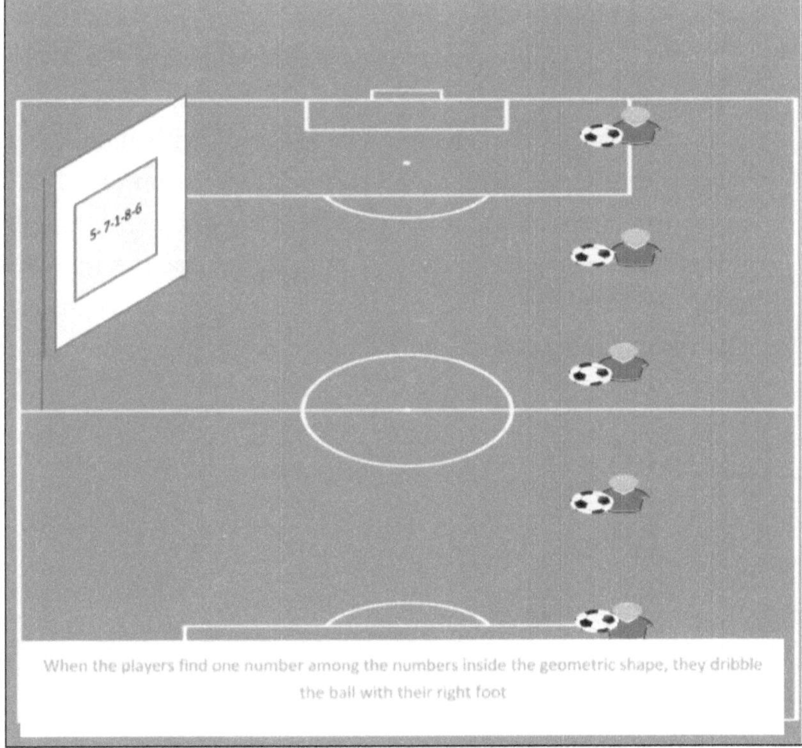

When the players find one number among the numbers inside the geometric shape, they dribble the ball with their right foot

> When the players find one number among the numbers inside the geometric shape, they dribble the ball with their right foot

Exercise (2) Exercise name: Distraction signals

Type of exercise: Mandatory technical exercise

The goal of the exercise: developing selective attention for players - developing passing with the sole of the foot

Tools and equipment: football field - footballs - whistle

Organization and preparation: Four players stand in a square, and in the middle of each square there is a defender. Each square holds one ball. Instructions: The player in possession of the ball in each square passes to the

player who points with the number one hand. The players move inside and on

the borders of the square while pointing with numbers with their hand to try to distract the player in possession of the ball. If two or three players point with the number one hand, the player in possession of the ball passes. To the player closest to him, just as the defending player in the middle of the square tries to extract the ball, the players in each square exchange passes in this way.

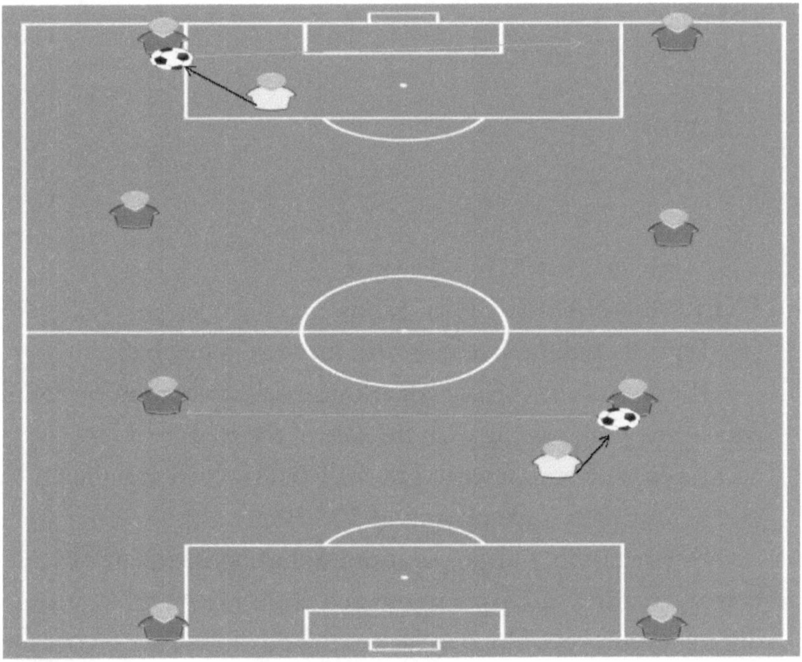

Exercise (3)

EXERCISE NAME: CHECK box

Type of exercise: Exercise with more than one ball

The goal of the exercise: developing selective attention for players - developing passing with the sole of the foot

Tools and equipment: Football field - two numbered balls (1:2) - lime for a square layout of 20 * 20 m

Organization and preparation: Standing in square (6) are attackers wearing uniforms numbered from (1:6) and defenders in different uniforms. The attackers with odd-shirts have possession of ball number one, and those with

even-shirts have possession of ball number two.

Instructions: The double-shirt players exchange the number two ball while trying to disperse the odd-shirt players throughFreedom of the type of passing

they make, as they have the freedom to pass with the sole of the foot, the front side of the foot, the outer side, and the inside of the foot. It is necessarySingle jersey players do the same thing as they take turns passing the ball number oneAs you doDouble-shirt players, as for the defenders, are free to press any group, whether double or odd, or both together.

32

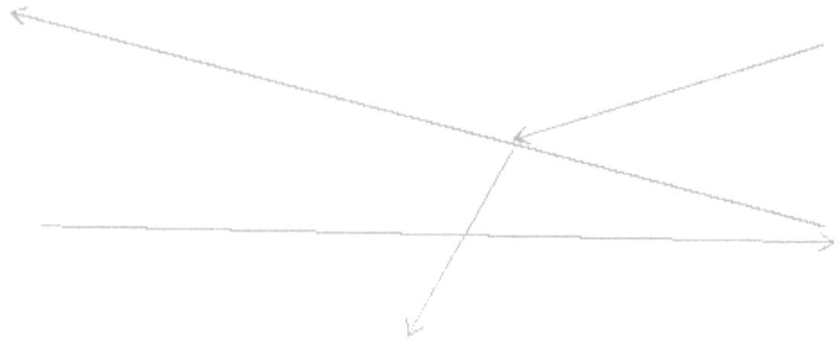

7

1

THE EXERCISE(4) EXERCISE name: Player numbers tasks

The goal of the exercise: developing selective attention for players - developing passing with the sole of the foot

Tools and equipment: soccer field - soccer ball - whistle

Organization and preparation: The players are divided into two teams, one team in red and the other in blue. Each team wears shirts numbered (1:7).

Instructions: At the start signal, the team that begins the attack exchanges

passes as follows(1:3)The ball is passed to them with the inside of the foot, the players from (6:4). The ball is passed to them with the outside of the foot, the playersfrom(9:7) The ball is passed to them with the inside foot facing. Each player passes when he takes possession of the ball in this way. The player who makes a mistake in passing loses his team the ball and becomes a defender.

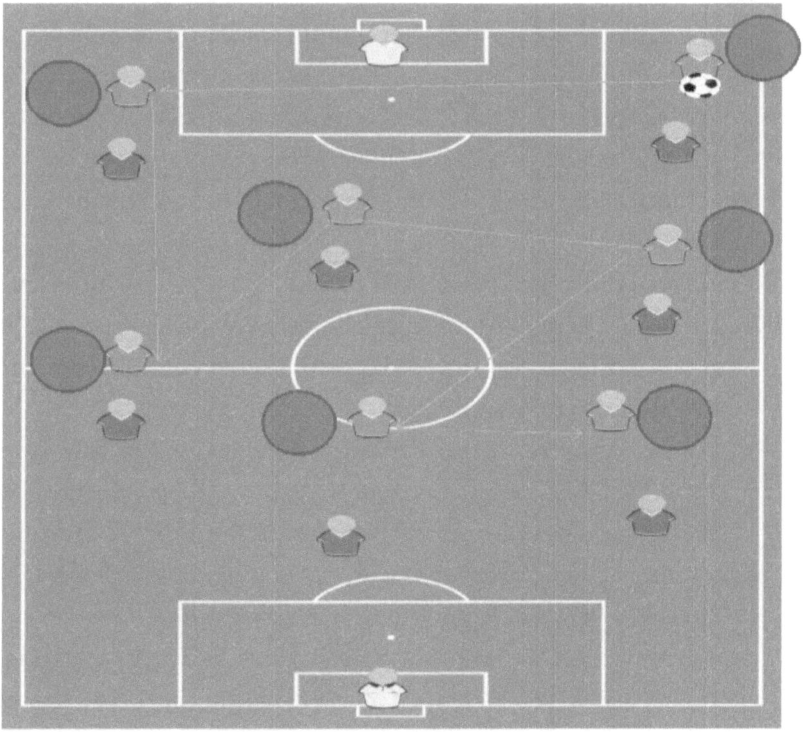

1

6

2

3

5

7 4

the exercise(4)

EXERCISE NAME: VOICE selection Exercise type: Mini-game exercise

The goal of the exercise: developing selective attention for players - developing passing with the sole of the foot

Tools and equipment: football field - footballs - audio recorder

Organization and preparation: The players are divided into two teams, each team7) Players, one team in red and the other team in blue.

Instructions: At the start signal, the team in possession of the ball attacks, paying attention to the voice recorder, which repeats numbers randomly in a good, slightly audible voice, as some numbers have tasks and the players are

aware of them before the match, while othersNumbers have no functionsIt has no tasks

For example, one number represents the task of shifting the attack to the sideleftFrom the field, number twenty-one diverts the attack to the sideRightThe number thirty-one is played in the depth of the field, and thus the performance is done by selecting the numbers that have tasks from among the numbers that the voice recorder says.

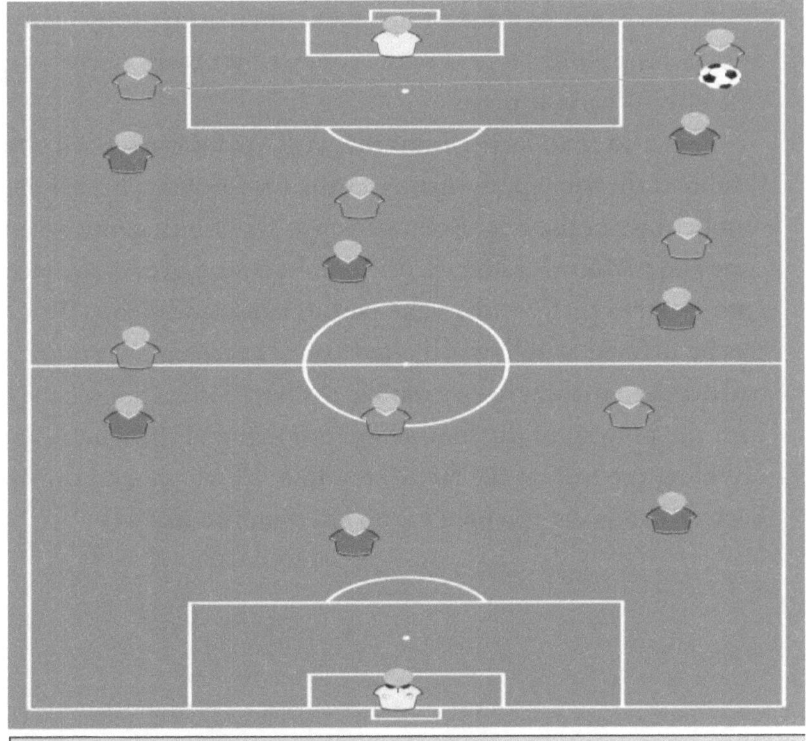

Exercise (1)

EXERCISE NAME: ALTERNATION set

The goal of the exercise: developing the alternating attention of the players - developing the sense of the ball

Tools and equipment: football field - colored cones - footballs

Organization and preparation: The coach places colored cones on the field freely spread across the field. The colors should be as follows (red, blue, white). The players are divided into two groups. The first is the rotation group, wearing the blue uniform, and the second is the rotation implementation group, wearing the red uniform.

Instructions: At the start signal, the alternating group performs by switching positions next to the cones, where each cone has a specific task. When the player

rests next to it, he performs that task. As for the second group, it follows the same performance as the first group, where if player number one in the first group performs By standing next to a red cone and performing his task, the number one player in the second group should perform the same performance, and so on. The tasks can be defined as follows: the red cone is exchanging passing the ball between the feet from running, the blue cone is pulling the ball with the bottom of the foot while running, and the white cone is dribbling the ball on the face of the foot, the thigh, and the head. Each task must be executed for no less than five seconds

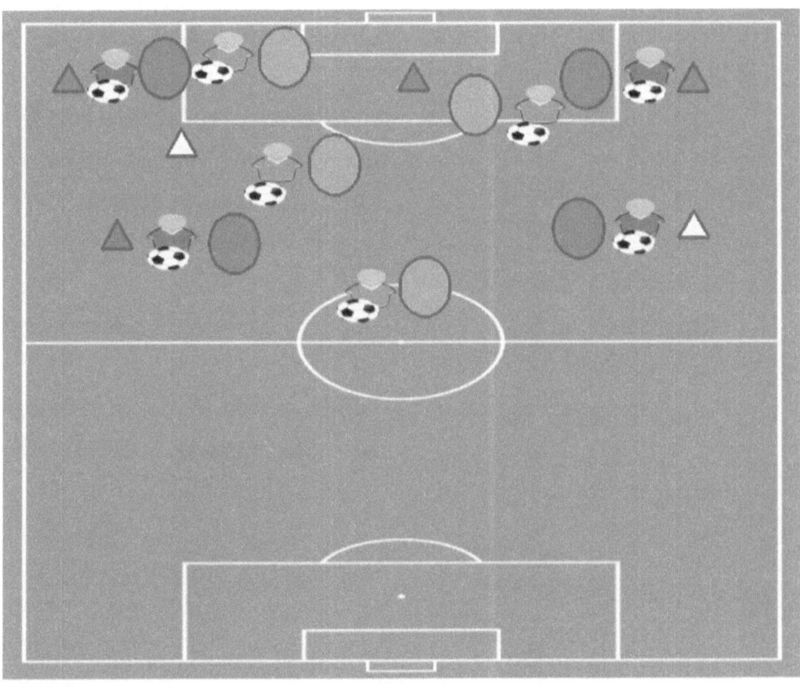

4 3

1

2

1

3

2

4

EXERCISE (2) EXERCISE name: Rotating displays

The goal of the exercise: developing the alternating attention of the players - developing the sense of the ball

Tools and equipment: football field - footballs - two display screens Organization and preparation: The coach selects a 25 x 25 m field. He installs a screen at a suitable height to the right of the field, and another to the left of

the field, where each screen displays a typeDifferentOn the other hand, let the screen on the right display imagesnumbersThe other screen displaysshapesThe duration of each screen change is one second. The players spread freely on the field, each player in possession of a football

Instructions: At the start signal, the players do different sensation exercises,

paying attention to what is shown on the two screens and saying it out loud. It is necessary not toHe ignoresPlayers can display anything on the two screens

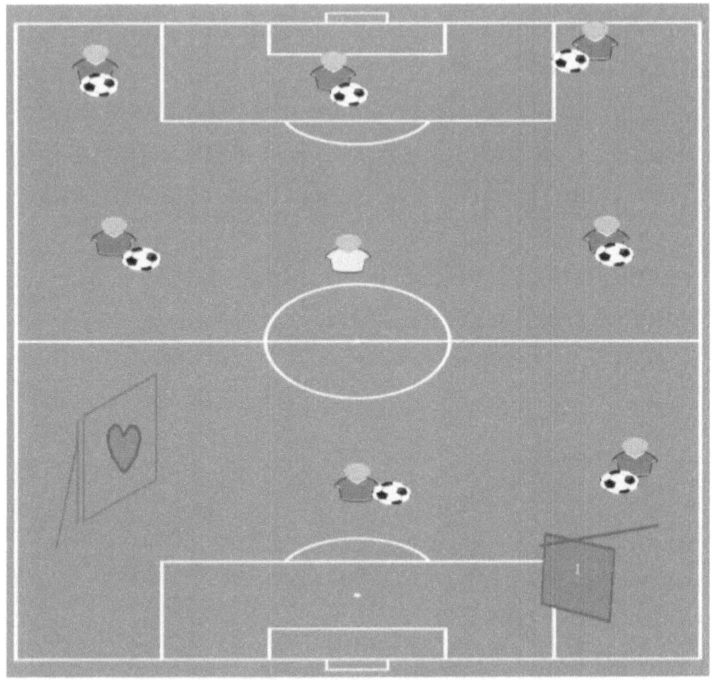

Exercise (3)

EXERCISE NAME: TASK shirts Exercise type: mini game

The goal of the exercise: developing players' alternating attention - developing passing with the sole of the foot

Tools and equipment: football field - footballs - numbered shirts Organization and preparation: Players wear shirts numbered (1:5). Players stand freely spread across the field. Each player is drawn to a football.

The coach assigns a task to each shirt number worn by the players as follows Shirt number one: The player dribbles the ball with his foot. Shirt number two: The player alternates pulling the ball with the bottom of the foot right and left. Shirt number three: The player alternates passing the ball between the feet.

Shirt number four: The player alternates touching the ball with the bottom of the foot. Shirt number five: The player exchanges By taking turns pulling the ball forward and backward with the bottom of the foot, all tasks must be free to spread and run on the field.

Instructions: The players exchange balls randomly and switch tasks. For

example, if player number five passes the ball to player number one, they must exchange tasks together.

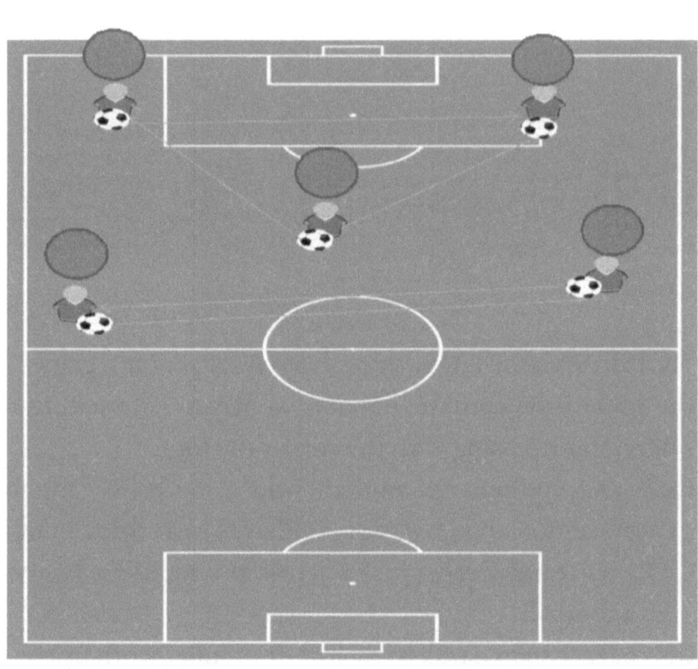

2 1

3
4

the chapterFifth

Develop slow thinking abilitiesFor football players

(B)Mental effort

The concept of mental effort

Humans are often called "cognitive misers" because of their aversion to mental effort. People inside and outside the laboratory often show preferences for low- effort tasks and are willing to forgo financial reward to avoid more demanding alternatives. However, mental effort does not seem to be avoided everywhere: people play crosswords, board games, and read novels, all as forms of entertainment. While such activities undoubtedly require effort, the type of cognitive demands they impose appear to be markedly different from the tasks typically used in psychological research on mental effort.AndThe idea that effort is aversive is intuitively attractive and has underpinned many important psychological theories. Originally, these theories were concerned with aversion to physical exertion (e.g., the law of least action, Hull, 1943), but when the focus of psychology shifted toward unobservable cognitive mechanisms, the law of least action was similarly applied to cognition (Kahneman), Awareness, this shows that many of the activities that we direct require mental effort and that some of the activities we can make mental effort while practicing them without getting bored or disgusted,

while others are in a state of aversion to exerting mental effort while practicing them, and this shows that mental effort is a combination. Of certain elements that cannot be separated from each otherThis is what we will discuss in the following pagesIt is necessary to pay attention to studying mental effort in order to find out how to develop it in players during training and competition so that we can stimulate their slow thinking.

The concept of mental effort : -

Mental effort was first used as a concept to help determine how hard a person is trying to effectively process the information presented. The mechanism was seen as a combination of the characteristics of perceived demand, perceived self-efficacy (personal experiences), and the level of depth of information processing with the first two influencing the latter which determines the amount of mental effort invested. The characteristics of perceived demand depend on the degree to which the source (e.g., stimulus, task, context) being attended to constitutes demands on a person's processing, because the information must be extracted, differentiated, remembered, and expanded upon.

Therefore, tasks that require concentration require mental energy to be expended in order to perform them. For example, if I ask you to solve the following problem without a calculator, 512 / 14 * 12 = ...

Naturally, you will recall the laws of arithmetic operations and then begin to solve them, which will make you need more concentration and thus exert greater effort than solving the following problem: 5 * 5 = ...

It will not take you more than five seconds to realize that the result is (25), and this shows that the characteristics of the task affect the degree of mental effort expended, as well as the perceived self-efficacy, which was represented here in the prior awareness of the multiplication table, which made you not late or exert a higher effort in order to Reaching the solution to the second issue.

But we must pay more attention to understanding the term (effort), as this term has more than one meaning in psychology.

The first meaning reflects the difficulty or complexity of the task. For example, running 400 meters requires greater physical effort than running 100 meters. Repeating a performance five times is more stressful than repeating it only twice. Likewise, solving a problem or performing a task that involves three variables is seen as requiring more mental effort than the related problem that includes, for example, only two variables. The concept of effort here is similar to the concept of work in physics. Therefore, the more difficult and complex the problem is, the more mental effort it requires, and this is what cognitive load research has shown Here, the cognitive load of the task must be proportional to the players' abilities in terms of working memory, which cannot perform multiple tasks that require mental effort at one time. For example, you cannot solve a complex mathematical problem while making a very important phone call at the same time. In which you are sitting in front of the television to watch a decisive match for your favorite team, the same applies when playing football. While you are defending against a strong and fast attack of the opposing team, you cannot hear, perceive and apply all the information that the coach says from outside the lines.

This is not a weakness in your attention abilities, but rather Because there is a task that requires greater mental effort, which is defending against attack, which requires intense concentration to realize the movements of the attackers and deal collectively with the defenders against the attack Therefore, when the cognitive load of the task exceeds the players' capabilities, it becomes an overload of the players' capabilities, and cognitive overload is a common thing. Because the capacity of working memory is limited, it cannot process only a small number of information at one time, and the information that we process inappropriately is quickly forgotten, and this shows us that it is necessary when planning training exercises to take into account the amount of new information so that it does not represent a burden on the mental effort of the players. For example, when you plan exercises to develop the types of players' attention, you must take into account the amount of stimuli that you place within one exercise. Likewise, when planning tactical exercises, they must be compatible with the players' cognitive abilities represented in the individual, pairs, and group tactical performance and the team as a whole. In many cases, we find the coach... Screaming outside the field as a result of some players not implementing the agreed-upon tactical performance.

One of the reasons why players do not implement the tactical performance is that the amount of information present in the tactical performance is disproportionate to the mental effort and working memory of the players, as the huge volume of new information is a common cause of overload, as many have confirmed. From studies.The quantity of information is not the only source of cognitive load during training and competition, as the cognitive load also increases through the quality of information, when the information is unfamiliar and more complex, or the speed of performance is higher than the physical capabilities of the players. This is also why, when planning football training, the number of variables present in football training must be taken into account. The training unit, as well as within a single exercise, as well as taking into account the degree of difficulty of these variables compared to the capabilities of working memory on the one hand and on the other hand the level of the players' physical, skill and tactical skills. It is also necessary to sequence the variables within the exercises throughout the training season because this makes the players more capable of dealing with the variables. New and more complex ones appear to them as if they are familiar, as they have previously been trained in similar situations, which allows players to provide feedback and make a good connection between new and old ideas,

which makes the players' task in dealing with new variables easier from a psychological and mental perspective, as the new information becomes somewhat familiar. They have even if they are complex or the speed of performance during the implementation of the exercises is higher than the physical capabilities of the players, and therefore one of the factors that will overcome the cognitive overload of the players, and it also makes the players more focused throughout the training season, is taking into account the quantity, type and sequence of the new variables. When planning training programs, starting from within a single exercise up to Olympic programs, since our slow thinking when working on a task that requires mental effort and at the same time with another task that can be performed on autopilot represented by quick thinking, multitasking is acceptable and does not affect It depends on our slow thinking abilities. For example, we can practice football training while listening to music, as the first task, which is football training, is called a primary task, as it requires an appropriate mental effort to perform it correctly, while the second task, which is listening to music, is called a secondary task, as it does not You need to make a mental effort due to hearing these songs before, or they are not as important to us in this situation as the first task. The same applies to training in basic skills.

For example, when learning the skill of visual scanning while performing an exercise for the skill of passing with the sole of the foot, the focus is On the primary task of good visual scanning, while scrolling with the sole of the foot becomes a secondary task due to your mastery of performing the skill under autopilot before. On the contrary, multitasking becomes difficult when we try to perform two or more tasks that require mental effort. For example, when we try to perform a set. Short passes in a narrow space with an organized defense.

Given that this task is complex and contains more than one task that requires mental effort, we may overlook good movements by a colleague on the other side of the field or not listen carefully to the instructions of the coach or colleague, given that the passes The short shot in the middle of the defensive block requires great mental effort in terms of understanding the movements and positions of the defenders and teammates, distances and the speed of the ball. In the end, all of this shows us that the quantity and quality of information in terms of the degree of difficulty and its occurrence would affect the performance of our slow thinking, whether negatively or if we are not able to employ it.

In the required manner that is commensurate with our mental capacity, or in the affirmative if we employ it well.

Here we give an example outside the sports environment, first to illustrate the importance of taking into account the quantity and type of sequence in the variables. For example, in the academic stages of education, the curriculum is developed on the basis of sequence according to the age stage and its characteristics in all aspects of development, especially mental development. For example, if you are a student in the fourth grade of the College of Physical Education. You were asked to create a training program in football for a class in the budding stage. This is the first time that you will conduct a training program. Although planning education programs for this class is not easy, as we know, you can simply remember a lot of information about this group. This category also at least has a general idea of how to plan training programs for such a category. Therefore, it is necessary that you have more information that has previously been studied about this category, such as that this category needs fun and happiness, and this category does not need theoretical explanation.

Also, this category has its physical aspect in the form of mini-games in certain proportions, and the training unit takes place in a short period of time commensurate with the age, physical condition, and growth of that category.

Thus, the information will come to your mind so that you can form a general picture of planning training programs for this category. We note this in this For example, he was carrying within him two variables, one of which was new, which was planning a training program for the buds class, and the other was old, which was information stored in a sequential form that was learned during your first three grades while studying in the College of Physical Education, which made the second variable familiar to you, and you did not feel strange in dealing with the requirements that it presented. It consists of creating a training program for a specific category of buds.

(Examples through football) First example:-

When you are playing, for example, in the center of defence, and due to the absence of a right-side defender, the coach informs you that you will occupy his place on the right side during the next match, which will be held within a week of course, and even if the coach intensifies the information, explanation

and training for you, your performance will not be the same as what you perform.

In your primary position, which is the center back, whether on the skill side in terms of coming up with the ball, passes, and defensive performance, or the tactical side, which is the reverse coverage with the center back, observing the team's defense from the left side, setting the offside line, linking up with your right winger, or entering deep into the field to make plays. Agreed collective plans as well, even on the physical side. Your poor judgment of the different playing situations during the match will cost you more obvious physical effort. All of this is due to the cognitive overload that you were exposed to while changing your position in a short period of time, represented by a week, which was imposed on you. The amount of information increased on one side, and on the other hand, the quality of the information was somewhat unfamiliar to you because you had not performed in this center before. Also, due to the lack of time, the sequence in training on the characteristics of this new center was not taken into account, and this was the result of fluctuation in skill performance and confusion in tactical performance. Physical effort doubles, making the idea of mental effort very exhausting and difficult .

Second example:

When a player moves to a new team that plays in a league that is stronger than the one he was in in terms of competition, performance, and fandom, we notice that he takes some time to get along with the team, as we notice in his first matches wrong movements and a large number of wrong passes as well, as well as the tactical aspect in terms of Connecting with colleagues during attack or defense is due to the fact that his physical, skill, tactical and mental capabilities are not proportional to the nature of the team's performance in terms of physical, skill, tactical and mental aspects. Here we do not mean the weakness of these aspects of the player, but rather that he moved from a lower level to a higher level with quantity and type of information. Increasing than before and new variables, which force the player to exert more physical and mental effort to fit into the team in a higher way. We can cite an example to clarify this, which is Portuguese coach Jose Mourinho's description of the Egyptian and international star Mohamed Salah that he was lonely, naive and physically fragile when he joined the team. Chelsea club, which was coached by Mourinho at the time, but Salah is no longer coached at the present time.

This came in a statement made by the Portuguese on beIN Sports, where adapting to a new reality with a team like Chelsea playing in the English Premier League is different from Basel, which plays in the Swiss League. In terms of competition, performance, and mental, physical, skill, and tactical requirements, but the talent that Salah possesses, whether on the physical side, such as speed of all kinds, or the basic, individual, and tactical skill aspects, and the mental aspect, which has developed very noticeably over the past years in terms of attention of all kinds and mental effort, which has become more efficient. You can discover this through the player's goal-making curve in recent years, which takes an ascending form, as well as his rate of possession of the ball, the number of touches, and the development of movements. This is in addition to the professional personality that the player possesses in terms of understanding his abilities and working to develop them, which made him a bright star in the sky of the English Premier League, but The question here is: Do all players have the ability to comprehend their abilities and the extent of their need for training within each training unit ?

Is it possible to plan training that helps players develop their mental effort ? ?

In the first part of the question, we find it difficult that all the players in one team have high scores in terms of understanding their abilities, especially mental ones, with regard to the efficiency of mental effort specifically, and this causes the player a great dilemma in understanding and applying basic and tactical skills during training and competitions. As for the second part. From the question, coaches can plan exercises that challenge the players' abilities in terms of the degree of difficulty and the number of variables, taking into account the sequence in the variables as well as the degree of difficulty so that this does not turn into an excessive cognitive load for the players, which hinders correct performance.

In the end, we can say that one of the factors affecting the first concept of mental effort, which is concerned with the degree of difficulty or complexity of the task, is the excessive cognitive load represented by the quantity and quality of information in terms of the number of new variables to which the player is exposed, whether in training within a single exercise, then within the training unit, and then during The training week, up to the Olympic program, and its type in terms of difficulty.Here are some examples of training planning to develop the mental effort of players according to the first concept of mental effort : -

the exercise (1) Exercise name: Arithmetic teacher

The goal of the exercise: developing the efficiency of the players' mental effort according to the first concept - developing passing with the sole of the foot Tools and equipment: soccer field - soccer balls

Organization and preparation: Four players stand in a square 25 x 25 m, with a

defender in the middle of each square. Each square holds one soccer ball. Instructions: Before any player passes the ball to one of his teammates, the defender makes a throwIssueMath on it like

50-7 = The player must solve the problem first and then pass the ball. It is

necessary to answer very quickly, and it is also necessary for the problems to be easy. The player cannot pass before solving the problem, and if he is late, this will cost him losing the ball through the defender who is working to retrieve the ball.

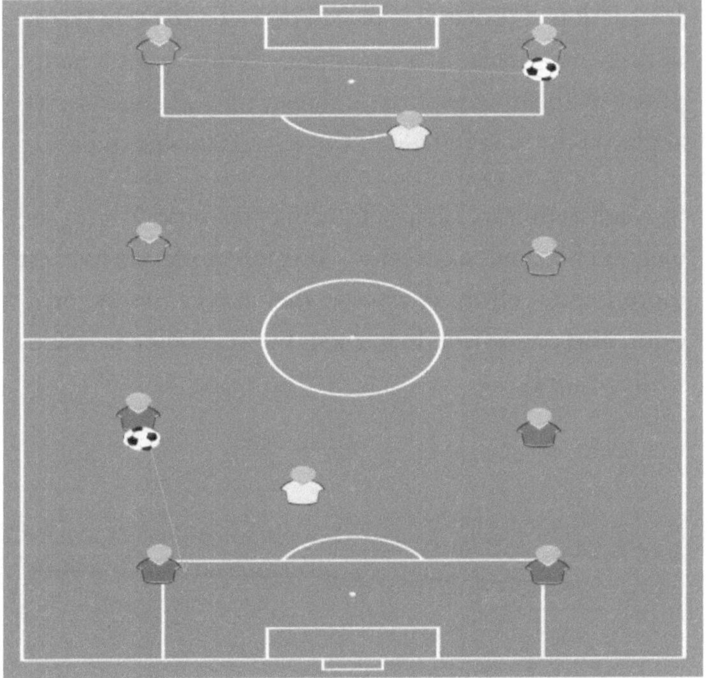

Exercise (2)

Exercise name : Geometric formation Exercise type : Mini-game exercise

The goal of the exercise: developing the efficiency of the players' mental effort according to the first concept - developing passing with the sole of the foot

Tools and equipment : soccer field - soccer ball - whistle

Organization and preparation: The players are divided into two teams, each team has (7) players

Instructions : A match is played between the two teams, lasting 5 minutes. The attacking team must exchange passes by forming geometric shapes such as a square, triangle, circle, or rectangle. If the team is unable to pass

through geometric shapes for thirty seconds, it loses the ball and becomes a defender. This forces players to exert more mental effort to choose the correct moves, positions, and passes that help them build geometric shapes while passing.

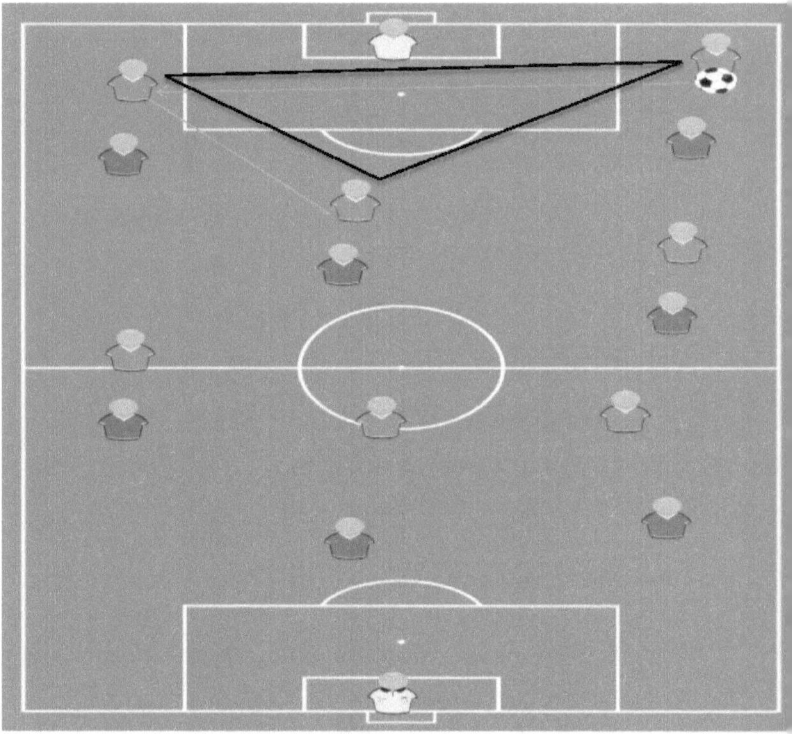

Exercise (2) Exercise name : Complex tasks

Exercise type : Mini-game exercise

The goal of the exercise: developing the efficiency of the players' mental effort according to the first concept - developing passing with the sole of the foot

Tools and equipment : soccer field - soccer ball - whistle

Organization and preparation : The players are divided into two teams, each team has (7) players. The coach must identify a player within each team whose task is to complicate the team's playing tasks. The player responsible for complicating the preparation and attacking process works to pass the

ball to the players within the team in positions, positions and movements that are difficult for them. What forces them to make a mental effort to solve these problems is that the players are forced to pass the ball to this player after each (3) Consecutive passes made by the team.

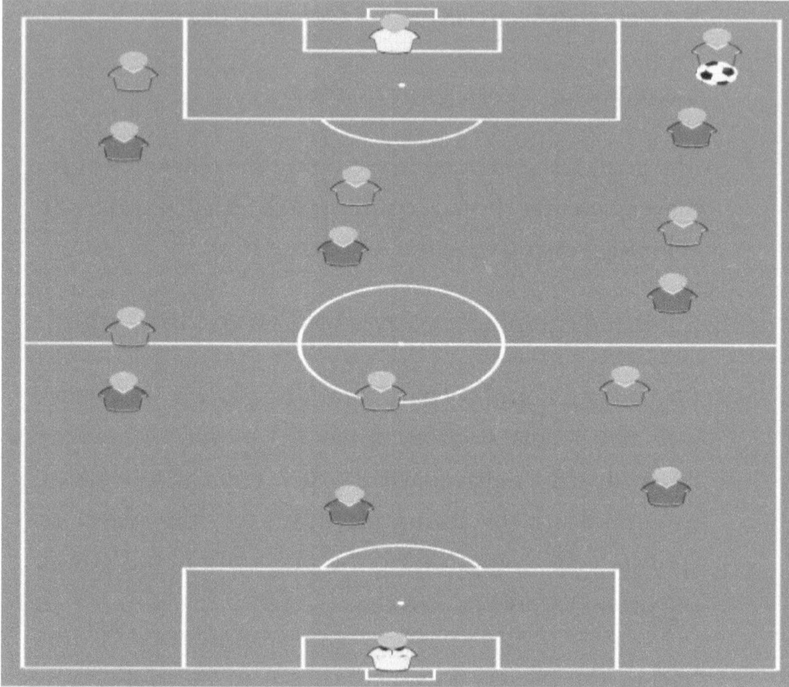

THE SECOND CONCEPT of effort refers to the extent to which a person is exposed to effort or aversion to carrying out the task. For example, when training for a specific tactical performance, players may feel that this performance is exhausting, annoying, or uncomfortable. This refers to emotional processing requirements that have a negative value when learning and training, and despite Therefore, frustration resulting from the effort expended is not required in itself in learning and practicing skills that require more mental effort during their performance, as it indicates motivational processes that are suboptimal, and this is why it is necessary when the tasks are seen as very complex from a theoretical point of view. Selfish or extremely disliked, it requires a certain type of optimism to face the difficulties found in these tasks, as when performing a task that requires great mental effort, it is like when we run a marathon and struggle to walk even a short distance, as there is physical fatigue, as well as tasks that require great mental effort. It affects our mood and concentration, and we feel that these tasks are arduous. Therefore, it is necessary to take into account, when planning and implementing training, the emotional state of the players in terms of feeling unmotivated, which may be due to the training not mobilizing the mental abilities of the players in the required manner and thus becoming like routine work, as well as the lack of focus. Which is often due to

the disproportionateness of the variables and the amount of information with the players' mental abilities, or it may be due to physical and health problems, as the player cannot reconcile physical effort with mental effort. As we mentioned previously, when the physical load exceeds the player's abilities, he becomes less focused or has social and psychological problems. Which is evident through the player's anger and annoyance easily, even if things do not require that nervousness, annoyance and anger. Through these points, you can know the reasons for the player not accepting the idea of mental effort, and based on them, we begin to deal with matters, since if the player is not prepared in the required manner, then the training will not take place. It is useful, even if it is set according to standards that are compatible with the player's mental abilities. The player must have the appropriate mental and psychological readiness to make a mental effort commensurate with the variables he is exposed to without that effort negatively affecting the player.

Therefore, this requires us, as we mentioned previously, to understand the nature of The mentality of the player and the psychological and social factors that would affect the efficiency of his mental effort, on the one hand, while the other aspect relates to the nature of the tasks and training that the coach plans. It is necessary that they suit the mental capabilities of the players and that they

take into account the principles of progression and individual differences, as well as the interconnection of training ideas throughout the season. Because in this way, the player feels that the new variables he has previously been exposed to throughout the season, and thus they are familiar to him and he accepts them better, even if they require great mental effort, as the old information and ideas provide even psychological and mental preparation for the new variables to which the player is exposed. For example, when you want to teach and train players the skill of running with the ball through basic skills training methods while developing the mental effort of the players, it is preferable for one exercise to pass in its basic form through all basic skills training methods, starting from sensation exercises to mini-games, while creating sub-variables on them. Practicing when moving from one method to another within the basic skills training methods in football, while linking this to the physical and tactical aspects throughout the training season.

Here is a model for planning a single exercise that will be generalized to all basic skills training methods in its basic form, with modifications in the quantity and type of variables: - For example, if we take (the geometric formation exercise that we mentioned in the first concept exercises in order to work through it on developing the second concept of mental effort We will maintain the basic structure of the exercise, which is the geometric formation required of the players during performance, and the benefit that the players receive from performing this exercise, while introducing some new variables and gradually increasing the difficulty of these variables during each method of training in the basic skills of football, starting with the method of training on football. Basic skills through ball sense exercises and even the method of training basic skills through mini-games. This can be done as follows. To clarify, this is a model to explain the idea. You, as a player or coach, can create different ideas based on the same model that I will list.

First exercise

Exercise name : Maze of geometric shapes Type of exercise : ball sensation exercise

The goal of the exercise : the efficiency of the players' mental effort according to the second concept of mental effort - developing the sense of the ball Tools and equipment : football field - colored cones - footballs - whistle

Organization and preparation : The players stand freely spread out on the field.

Each player is given a football. The coach places a large number of colored cones freely spread out on the field, provided that the distances between the cones are unequal.

Instructions : The players do sensation exercises by running and moving on the

field. The players must make three different geometric shapes during each minute of the exercise time, and each shape must be made.aGeometric shapes by positioning the players next to cones of a uniform color. For example, if they want to make a circle, they must determine the color first, let it be white, then make a circle by positioning each player towards a white cone in the appropriate place to build a circle shape. This increases the focus of the players and requires them to approach and understand each other. mentality among them

The second exercise Exercise name : Forced formation

Type of exercise : Mandatory technical exercise

The goal of the exercise : developing the efficiency of the players' mental effort according to the second concept of mental effort - developing passing with the sole of the foot

Tools and equipment : soccer field - soccer ball - whistle

Organization and preparation : The coach determines a field with an area of 20 x 20 m. The coach plans a group of geometric shapes overlapping on the field. The number of players is (7) players wearing numbered shirts with the presence of defenders.

Instructions : Scrolling between them is as follows

Players with individual shirts (1, 3, 5, 7) pass through geometric shapes (triangle, square

They receive through geometric shapes (rectangle, circle).

Players with even shirts (2, 4, 6) pass through the shapes (rectangle, circle) They signify receipt through geometric shapes (triangle, square).

Third exercise Exercise name: Speed formation

Type of exercise: Training in basic skills through physical attributes

The goal of the exercise: developing the efficiency of the players' mental effort according to the second concept of mental effort - developing passing with the

sole of the foot

Tools and equipment: football field - soccer ball - whistle

Organization and preparation: The coach determines a field with an area of 20 x 20 m. The coach places a group of cones on top of each side the field, provided that the cones on each side of the field are of a uniform color and are as follows: the first side is red cones, the second side is yellow cones. The third side has blue cones, the fourth side has green cones, dividing the players into

(6) attackers and (2) defenders.

Instructions: The coach asks the attackers to make (4) geometric shapes while holding the cones while passing and determining the geometric shape. This is done within a time frame determined by the coach, let it be (3) minutes.

This means that the defenders try to extract the ball from the attackers and try to prevent them from completing geometric shapes through defense and pressure

Fourth exercise Exercise name: Mandatory single and double formation Type of exercise: Exercise with more than one ball

The goal of the exercise: developing the efficiency of the players' mental effort

according to the second concept of mental effort - developing passing with the sole of the foot

Tools and equipment: Football field - two numbered balls (1:2) - whistle

Organization and preparation: The coach determines a field with an area of 25 x 25 m. He divides the players into (7) attackers who possess two numbered balls and (2) defenders.

Instructions: At the start signal, the attacking players exchange passes as

follows

Ball No. (1) The players take turns passing it among themselves through one of the formations, a square, a triangle.

Ball number two. The players take turns passing it among themselves through formations, a circle, a rectangle

The defenders' task is to extract the ball from the attackers. The attacker from whom the ball is extracted becomes a defender, and so on

Fifth exercise

Exercise name: White suppression is prohibited Type of exercise: Complex physical skill exercise

The goal of the exercise: developing the efficiency of the players' mental effort according to the second concept of mental effort - developing passing with the sole of the foot

Tools and equipment: football field - colored cones - football - whistle -

stopwatch

Organization and preparation: The coach determines a field with an area of 25 * 25 m. The coach places on the field a group of colored cones freely spread across the field. He divides the players into (7) attackers and (2) defenders.

Instructions: The coach sets a time for the attackers, let it be a minute, to create a geometric shape by passing and positioning next to the cones. This is provided that the geometric shape that the attackers make does not

include one of the white cones at the same time that the defenders are trying to extract the ball from the attackers. This is what imposes on the players more From focusing on reading the field and the positions and passes they make in order to do so, the time element also represents a burden on the attackers, and this is what makes the players challenge their mental and volitional abilities.

Basic exercise

Exercise name: One figure Exercise type: mini game

The goal of the exercise: developing the efficiency of the players' mental effort according to the second concept of mental effort - developing passing

with the sole of the foot

Tools and equipment: soccer field - soccer ball - whistle

Organization and preparation: The players are divided into two teams of (8) players each, and a ten-minute match is played between them

Instructions: The team that is able to build and end the attack through a single geometric shape with multiple spaces and directions will be credited

with a goal even if no goal is scored.

AFTER COMPLETING THE exercise on all basic skills training methods, we can list the number of variables and the general benefit from preserving the basic elements of the exercise in all basic skills training methods.

Types of variables that were used in the exercise: The basic element is the method of solving problems in the training. Then we introduced into it the basic performance variables in terms of space, time, and mandatory restrictions, and linked them to mental effort. We can summarize the positive returns from the exercise in the following:

In the beginning, we created a very simple form of exercise through the method of feeling the ball, which is for the player to feel the importance of mental effort, and this is the first variable. Then we moved to a new variable, which is for the player to feel that in order to achieve a specific goal, he must accept the idea of mental effort and follow it through mental fatigue and impact. Psychologically and physically, and you have the ability to accept that in a better way.

THEN WE MOVED TO A third variable, which is how the player can make a quick change in the process of mental effort according to performance variables. The fourth variable is how the player can strike a balance between mental and physical effort and realize the importance of mental effort, the variable. The fifth is how the player can reach the highest efficiency of his mental efforts.

The third concept of effort refers to the initiation, intensity, and continuation of behavior associated with learning and training as a direct result of momentary stimulation. Therefore, it refers to the allocation of self-efforts made by players to deal with the requirements present within the training tasks, and this depends on the motivation present in the player, where the player is willing to make a certain effort. During training, when he has sufficient motivation, that is why value expectations related to performing a specific training task greatly determine the degree of mental effort expended, and that is why the third concept is extremely important, as coaches must, when planning training exercises, maximize the role of those training exercises in developing the players' level and clarify that. In theory before the performance and practically when the players begin to perform, the role and importance of the exercise must be clarified so that good motivations can be created for the players that help them continue to exert mental effort with good efficiency during the performance, and so that the coach can know the level of motivation among the players to make mental efforts to perform the exercise, he can direct the players to some Questions during the theoretical explanation, such as: What is the importance of this exercise for you ?

Can you perform this exercise well ?

Also, during the practical performance, you can ask some questions, such as Do you have the ability to continue performing well until the end of the exercise ?

Can you perform this exercise under higher defensive pressure than that ? Can you perform the exercise faster than that without making mistakes ?

After completing the performance of the training unit in general, you can make forms containing all the exercises in the unit. This is provided that none of the players write his name on the form so that he can comment very freely so that the coach is encouraged to identify the problems that hinder the players' mental effort in the exercises that the coach sets. Where the trainer can address problems in general.

Among the questions that can be asked in the form are Does this exercise help you develop your performance ?

Did the exercise motivate you to a good extent? Can you put a percentage? To what degree do you think you were focused during the performance ?

What is the benefit of this exercise for you ? Did you feel bored when performing ?

To what extent do you think this exercise is good for developing your performance ?

And other questions through which you can evaluate the exercises you plan and whether they motivate the players

We did not draw the last set of exercises, given that you no longer need the image of the exercise to understand it. You do as well. In your opinion, what type of thinking does this situation represent and what is the name of the characteristic that describes it ?

You can answer the book reviews

In this version of the book, we were able to take a fleeting look at the nature of the work of our mental functions,

whether in life situations in general or in football in particular. Let us consider this to be the beginning, as we will continue talking about how to develop quick thinking in football.

Please, after reading the book, evaluate it so that we can identify the good points and the points that need to be modified. Without you, I will not be able to know that. I hope I did not waste your time.

List of garagesA

1. - The Power of Your Subconscious Mind, written by Dr. Joseph Murphy, Jarir Bookstore

2. - The Power of the Subconscious Mind by Dr. Ibrahim Al-Faqi, Thammarat for Publishing and Distribution

3. – The Power of Positive Thinking, Norman Vincent Peale, House of Culture

4. – Thinking Fast and Slow by Daniel Kahneman, Hindawi Publishing Company

5. - The Invisible Gorilla, Christopher Chabris and Daniel Simons, translated by Omar Fayed, Page Seven Publishing and Distribution

6. - Cognition and the development of style: A new model of the mind. London: Routledge Press

7. - Patterns A. (2005). Attention, perception, and memory: An integrated production. New York: Psychology Press

1. Cognitive load and cognitive effort, Catherine Anne, Andrea Hunziker Heib, Zurich University of Applied Sciences

2. The book The Cognitive Burden between Theory and Application, Dr. Muhammad Youssef Al-Zoghbi, Nour Library

3. William James, Principles of Psychology (1890), New York: Henry Holt. pp. 404-403

Johnson A (2004) Cognitive Psychology and Its Implications (6th ed.). Worth Publishing House, p. 519.-11

1. https://www.midfitihypnosis.com/what-is-/the-subconscious-mind[1]

2. https://www.learnminddpower.com/using-/mind-power/the-subconscious-[2] synchronicity

---

1. http://www.midfitihypnosis.com/what-is-/the-subconscious-mind

2. http://www.learnminddpower.com/using-/mind-power/the-subconscious-

Don't miss out!

Visit the website below and you can sign up to receive emails whenever KASIM FARRAG publishes a new book. There's no charge and no obligation.

https://books2read.com/r/B-A-LIAMC-AOAAF

BOOKS 2 READ

Connecting independent readers to independent writers.

Also by KASIM FARRAG

Thinking Fast and Slow in Football

Watch for more at https://www.amazon.com/dp/B0DB8HPPJS.

About the Author

Football coach and author of coaching and sports psychology books. Author of the book The Comprehensive Mental Training Methodology in Football and the book Thinking, Fast and Slow in Football.

Read more at https://www.amazon.com/dp/B0DB8HPPJS.

www.ingramcontent.com/pod-product-compliance
Lightning Source LLC
Chambersburg PA
CBHW021425150726
47989CB00001B/119